THE ESSENTIAL
TEQUILA & MEZCAL
COMPANION

THE ESSENTIAL
TEQUILA & MEZCAL
COMPANION

HOW TO SELECT, COLLECT & SAVOR AGAVE SPIRITS

TESS ROSE LAMPERT

U

UNION
SQUARE
& CO.

NEW YORK

UNION SQUARE & CO.

NEW YORK

ISBN 978-1-4549-4540-6 (hardcover)
ISBN 978-1-4549-4541-3 (e-book)

Library of Congress Control Number: 2022942923

For information about custom editions, special sales, and premium purchases,
please contact specialsales@unionsquareandco.com.

Printed in China

2 4 6 8 10 9 7 5 3 1

unionsquareandco.com

Interior design by Christine Heun
Cover photo by Ludmila Meshcheriakova/Shutterstock.com
Image credits on page 290

Previous: Agave field for Rey Campero in Candelaria Yegolé,
Oaxaca, Mexico. **Opposite:** Vinata El Malpais, Durango.

This book is dedicated to the
many communities across Mexico
that have so generously shared
their culture with me.

CONTENTS

CHAPTER 1

INTRODUCTION

CHAPTER 2

TASTING 101

HOW TO USE THIS BOOK

This book is designed as a companion for those who are curious and passionate about agave spirits, those who indulge in the flavors and want to know the stories behind them. Unique in the world of spirits on many accounts, there is so much to learn, consider, and understand about these often majestic and flavor-packed elixirs. The information within this book is offered as a practical tool to aid you on a journey of discovering which spirits you enjoy the most, why, and how to select and serve the spirits that best align with your tastes.

The introductory information provides a landscape to understand the current world of tequila and mezcal, including the key elements that dictate flavor and style. There is a ton of variation in the world of agave spirits; digging into these nuances, especially through understanding agave's terroir—a fancy word to describe how a product can convey its unique origin—will allow you to choose the spirits that you will enjoy most thoroughly.

The meat of this book is producer profiles with tasting notes and general comments. Aside from serving as an at-a-glance overview of specific products, they offer insight into house production styles, flavor profiles for different agave varieties, and regionally specific characteristics. In addition to general comments and information, the tequila entries each get an individual score from 1 to 5. These ratings are designed to serve as a guide and inform consumers about the good, better, and best bottles in terms of quality and value, and, equally important, which bottles you might want to skip.

The cocktail recipes and pairing guides are there to help you find new ways to enjoy your carefully selected agave spirits. Many of the recipes come from established and emerging mixologists, who understand trends in the beverage industry and know how best to highlight the complexity found in these unique spirits.

Opposite: Loading the *horno* for a batch of mezcal by La Medida, in Miahuatlán de Porfirio Díaz, Oaxaca.

If you come across unfamiliar words or expressions, please reference the glossary of terms (page 278) as needed for definitions and explanations. There are multiple terms used to denote the same thing (for example: *palenque* and *vinata* may both be used interchangeably with distillery, depending on the region), as well as terms that can be used to denote different things (*mezcal*, for example, may refer to agaves in a field, cooked agaves, or the resulting spirit). I have done my best to use the words that are typical to each region and producer in an effort to reflect the inherent diversity and provide opportunities for education.

After digesting all of the information here, you may consider yourself an educated amateur able to make informed decisions about which spirits to buy and consume. But know that even after fifteen years dedicated to the category, I do not consider myself an expert; the experts have always been, and will always be, the people and communities that have been producing these spirits for generations. There is so much richness in the culture of agave beyond what you can read in a book or taste from a bottle.

A NOTE TO THE READER

As part and parcel of a living culture, agave spirits are much more than mere products to be enjoyed. We cannot separate our enjoyment of these liquors from the impacts our enjoyment have on communities that produce them across Mexico. Reflecting on the effects of our consumerism is increasingly important in all areas of life, and this is especially highlighted in the context of tequila and mezcal.

This book is not meant to serve as an overview of the cultural context or importance of agave and its spirits. With guidance from my Oaxacan and Mexican colleagues and friends, I have included a lengthy reference guide so that you may learn about the culture of mezcal, including mythology, history, and current issues, directly from the people claimed by the culture. I strongly encourage everyone to jump into that list of resources; it will no doubt increase your appreciation of every sip.

That said, my elevator pitch to those who seek to engage in enjoying tequila and mezcal in a way that minimizes harm is this: spend more on fewer bottles, ideally on producer-owned brands. Of course, it goes much deeper than this, but this is a good place to start. Agave spirits demand a more informed customer than many other beverages and foods, and as we embrace that call to educate ourselves, it can serve as a template of how to engage more deeply with other goods we consume.

The landscape of agave spirits is dynamic and rapidly changing. This book was written in 2021, in the midst of global turmoil, and reflects the state of the industry during that time.

With this in mind, I hope this book will help you choose bottles that are so special they seem to speak directly to your soul.

Opposite: Jimador Guillermo Hernandez Rodriguez at the Gonzalez family fields, one of the fields of Tequila Siete Leguas.

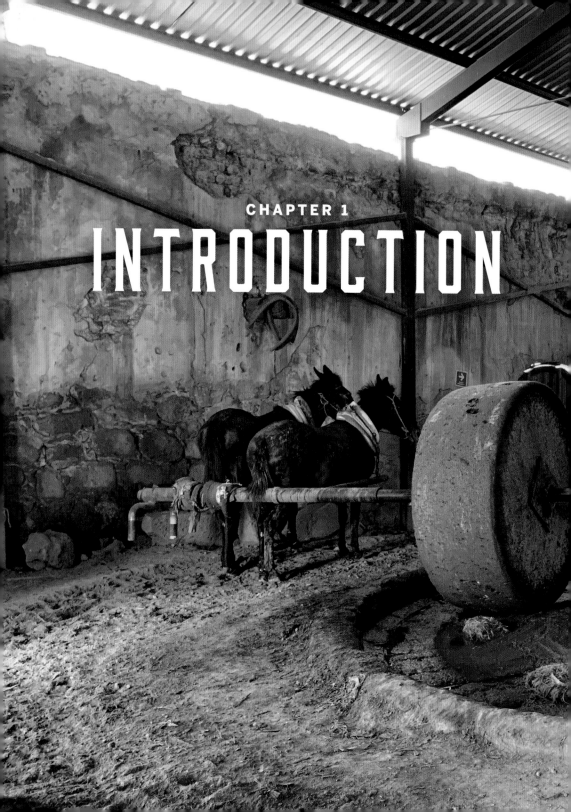

CHAPTER 1

INTRODUCTION

L ike so much in life, the true origins of mezcal are shrouded in mystery. Learning to accept this is essential, especially when it comes to thinking about what kind of distillation may have been happening before colonization. There is evidence based on research from the National Autonomous University of Mexico (UNAM) that points to distillation of agave between 693 and 878 BCE, showing that agave distillation was part of Mesoamerican culture at least 2,500 years ago. Other research shows the use of a unique small clay still, called a Capacha vessel, with remnants of agave that date back to 1500 BCE. There are also references from the written records of Domingo Lázaro de Arregui, author of *Description of the New Galicia*, in the early 1600s that describe a local tradition of a "distilled wine" that is "clear as water" and "stronger than aguardiente [brandy]." As research continues more evidence is coming to light that points to some type of Indigenous distillation tradition, albeit it is different from how the spirits are produced today.

What is indisputable is that the distillation technology presented by Europeans, learned from other cultures, catapulted the world of agave spirits into a new age. The introduction of elements such as millstones operated by horse, donkey, or mule; copper stills; and aboveground ovens are some of the elements that ushered tequila into a more mainstream and widely available beverage. The thirst of the colonizers, despite the Spanish attempt to prohibit mezcal, is another factor that ushered in an age of mezcal as a social beverage, in addition to its uses in medicinal and spiritual contexts.

Given the vast knowledge of the Indigenous people for using the plant in so many ways, it is logical to hypothesize their desire to distill this life-giving and culturally important plant into a pure concentrated form. It is more likely that the myth perpetuated by colonizers, that Indigenous inhabitants of the land were less civilized and knowledgeable than their European counterparts, led to a premature conclusion that distillation was beyond their capabilities.

Previous: The *tahona* in action at Hacienda Peñasco San Luis Potosí, which produces mezcal for Pal'alma. **Opposite:** Agave plant.

Those who wish to explore this subject further can find a list of resources in the reference guide (page 284).

Tequila & Mezcal: What's the Difference?

When it comes to agave spirits, the most common misperception is that mezcal is tequila's smoky cousin. If we want to use a family analogy, mezcal would be tequila's great-grandmother and matriarch of the family. As we'll discover in more depth later in this book, mezcal is the origin of all agave spirits, and tequila is one subvariety of mezcal that happened to take off in popularity and rise to fame because of historical and sociopolitical reasons, a subject that has entire books devoted to it.

These key factors below describe why the flavors of tequila and Mezcal are fundamentally different. Of course, there are more differences, not least of which is the unique culture that surrounds each spirit. Aspects like wood aging practices, regulations, and trends are also different when it comes to tequila and Mezcal. Since agave spirits are terroir-driven by nature, many of these more subtle distinctions appear on a case-by-case basis.

Today, tequila and Mezcal still share a lot in common as agave-based spirits from Mexico, but there are key differences that describe how and why they are different. Here are the three big factors that set these spirits apart.

Note: **Throughout this book the word** *mezcal* **can be understood to encompass all agave spirits from Mexico unless a distinction is being made, while the capitalized word Mezcal will be reserved for the legally protected status of a certain subset of agave spirits.**

GEOGRAPHY

Tequila is mostly a regional spirit that takes its name from the place it comes from. The town of Tequila is in the state of Jalisco and has become so famous for its namesake spirit that the town itself is something of an amusement park for tequila, the beverage, complete with barrel-shaped trolleys to shuttle thirsty tourists from the town square to tequila factories. Legally, tequila can also be produced in the neighboring states of Guanajuato, Michoacán, and Nayarit, as well as Tamaulipas all the way over in the other corner of Mexico. Still, 95% of tequila comes from in and around the town of Tequila.

Traditional mezcal was produced long before governing bodies put laws in place to regulate it. Both what would culturally be considered mezcal and Mezcal, according to current laws, come from all over Mexico. In fact, the denomination of origin, or legally protected area of production for mezcal, is the largest such area designation in the world and covers a massive territory. With an exponentially larger territory, the variety of traditions, materials, and ultimately flavors is more ample in the Mezcal category.

PRODUCTION PROCESS

The first thing people usually notice about mezcal versus tequila is the presence of a smoky flavor. This smokiness comes from a key step in the process that is typically different for tequilas and other mezcals.

The hearts of the agaves, or *piñas*, must be cooked during production of both spirits. For tequila, the piñas are cooked in brick or steel ovens and essentially steamed, which does not impart any external flavor to the raw materials. For mezcal, it is traditional to cook the piñas in an in-ground pit, which looks like a cone-shaped hole in the ground. This process of building a firepit and using it to cook the piñas imparts a smokiness to the materials that results in the signature smokiness in the final spirit.

Another element of production that sets the two apart is the bottling proof. Tequila, for the most part, has followed along with other standard liquors and is usually bottled at or around 80 proof, or 40% alcohol by volume (ABV). Traditional mezcal, on the other hand, is traditionally bottled around 90 to 100 proof. Many mezcals that are bottled at or closer to 80 proof break with strict tradition in order to appeal to drinkers who want a softer, more approachable entry into the world of mezcal. It is worth mentioning that lower-proof mezcal is common and preferred in some regions throughout Mexico and can be quite tasty when made by an experienced distiller.

The addition of smokiness plus the additional flavors that come with a higher-proof spirit are two of the characteristics that result in mezcal having more flavor in the glass.

Opposite: Agaves cook in a brick oven at El Centenario distillery. **Above:** An *horno* being filled with *piñas*, using *pencas* as a protective layer between the hot rocks. La Luna Mezcal recycles the cooked *pencas* to feed to their cattle.

SELECTION OF PLANT SPECIES

By law tequila is made from one—and only one—variety of agave: Blue Weber Tequilana. It is a variety known for its high sugar content and early ripening qualities. Traditional mezcal, on the other hand, can be made from any variety of agave. There are over two hundred scientifically documented species of agave, of which thirty to fifty are used to produce Mezcal. This difference highlights the fact that tequila is one subvariety of the larger category of mezcal, similar to how California Cabernet is one subvariety of the larger category of wine.

Last, but not least, is that tequila can legally be made with 51% agave and include up to 49% other base materials, which is typically sugar cane spirit. This less-expensive style of tequila is called *mixto* and it is very popular, despite the backlash it receives from purists. Mezcal, on the other hand, must be made from 100% agave, no exceptions.

KEY DIFFERENCES AT A GLANCE

TEQUILA	MEZCAL
Regional spirit	Produced all over Mexico
Steamed	Cooked underground (smoky)
Standard proof (40% ABV)	Higher proof (45–55% ABV)
Blue agave only	Any agave variety
Mixto (up to 49% non-agave allowed)	100% agave

Agave: An Ancient & Noble Plant

Agaves come in many shapes and sizes. Imagine the succulent display at the garden store, and now imagine all of them as huge plants as big as and bigger than humans. Some are round and squat, while others are tall and oblong. All of them feature long leaves of varying widths that have spines along the edges.

The common name *agave* is derived from a Greek word for "noble" or "industrious," pointing to the value of the plant. The Indigenous names, including *maguey* and *metl* can be used interchangeably with agave. Making appearances throughout Indigenous mythology and depicted in ancient texts, these plants have been used by populations of the Americas for at least ten thousand years. The uses for agaves include food and beverage, medicine, building materials, hunting tools, textiles, and much more. There are accounts of women anointing the aguamiel, or sweet sap, on the lips of babies who wouldn't nurse, which provided essential amino acids to survive. There are communities today that continue to extract the fibers of agaves to make textiles and ropes. Sisal, a material you can buy at any hardware store, is made from agave fibers. While many people are rediscovering the majesty of agave through distilled spirits, it is a plant that has offered humanity so much.

LIFE CYCLE

Agaves are endemic to the Americas, and there are hundreds of species of agaves, of which around forty are used for making spirits. Multiple subcategories and subvarieties exist that vary greatly in terms of shape, size, and appearance. Scientifically classified as succulents, agaves are composed of four major parts: roots, heart, leaves or pencas, and a flowering stalk or quiote. Agaves take between six and thirty years to mature, requiring an investment of time and labor, unlike any other spirit or alcoholic beverage.

When an agave reaches maturity, it will send up its quiote from the center of the heart. In most cases this stalk will be cut down if the agave is destined to be distilled; this is typically called *capón*. This is done to keep the plant from sending its stored energy (sugars) to the stalk to grow and produce flowers and eventually seeds, but instead keeping its stored energy in the heart of the plant. Many varieties can reproduce without seed by way of rhizomatic pups that shoot off from the roots and pop up close to the mother plant. These are known as *hijuelos*. If the quiote is left to grow and flower, baby plants (*bulbils*) may grow directly from the flowering stalk, and these may also be referred to as hijuelos. Every variety has different tendencies, but as a group, agaves can reproduce sexually through seed as well as via root offshoots and bulbils from the quiotes, though not all varieties reproduce in all ways. Only plants that are started from seed are genetically unique; otherwise, they are clones of the mother plant.

Like most plant groups, there are at least two names for any given plant: the scientific name and the common name. Common names vary by region and can be applied to more than one variety. There can also be more than one common name for a specific variety. The scientific name is the only one that is guaranteed to be unique to a particular variety or subvariety; however, many different subvarieties may share a scientific name.

For example, *cenizo* means ashen or ashy and is a common name for many different varieties of agave throughout different regions; however, *Cenizo durangensis* is the scientific name for the most common variety of the state of Durango. Technically, anything other than *Cenizo durangensis* should not be called cenizo on a label—but that is unrealistic given that the common names are used colloquially. Similarly, there are many different varieties known simply as *verde*, which means green (you can guess why). When it comes to scientific names, it is the other side of the same coin: the scientific variety *Angustifolia* applies to the most common variety used to make mezcal—espadín, as well as a hyper regional subvariety from Sonora called *pacifica*. My best advice is not to get too bogged down with the scientific and regional names. If and when you are tasting from a specific region, focus on the regional names of the varieties to see if there is one or more that stands out to you. Even if you don't know the scientific name, knowing that the verde from a particular town is something you enjoy is more practical information than memorizing and cross-referencing scientific names with an endless list of variations of common or regional names.

AGAVES IN THE WILD AND IN THE FIELD

Agaves used for making spirits were traditionally harvested from the wild. Indigenous agriculture uses a system that includes crop rotation and allowing land to go fallow so that there is a plentiful supply of wild-growing species for harvest. The concept of estate-grown agaves or owning private fields of agave is largely new. Also, traditionally, agaves used for spirits were not harvested during rainy seasons, as this yields bloated agaves that have a lower concentration of sugars. In many regions, agave spirits are still made seasonally, avoiding harvest during rainy seasons. Wild agaves are also still harvested for spirit making, though the majority of tequila and mezcal is typically produced from cultivated plants on now privatized land. Agaves are typically planted in rows, and there are massive plantations of agaves in Jalisco for tequila and in Oaxaca for Mezcal. Cultivating agaves is not just for large operations; many small producers also now cultivate small- and medium-size plantations. There is a third method, called semi-cultivation, that relies on nurseries for seed and clonally propagated plants that are replanted in their wild habitat. Because of overharvesting and a growing demand for agave spirits, it is likely that within a generation or two, 99% of wild agave mezcal will be made from these semi-wild, semi-cultivated plants. This system is largely responsible for rescuing some of the rarer varieties from extinction altogether.

SUSTAINABILITY

The explosion of demand and production of agave spirits raises a long list of issues that affect the environment, including pollution from by-products, overharvesting of natural materials, and agave plantations displacing other native species and people that are important to the ecosystem, to name just a few. While many brands tout their commitment to replant three agaves for every one they harvest, deforestation as a consequence of clearing fields to plant additional agaves is a more serious climate concern. In Oaxaca, the exponentially growing lack of access to water will be the most pressing environmental concern in the coming generations. It is mostly organizations that are not affiliated with agave spirit brands that are raising awareness and taking action.

Intertwined with the environmental concerns is the equally pressing issue of cultural sustainability. There is a tendency to overromanticize the culture and practices of mezcal that often dehumanizes the people who make it—for example, conflating the humble distillery of a producer with the quality of their mezcal. Mezcal that is made in a dilapidated shack without a floor is not better because it is rustic—it is simply the reality of that producer, and it is their experience and expertise that creates a superior product, not their limited resources. Another element that threatens cultural sustainability is the influx of outsiders forcing their way into the industry, who believe that with enough money one can buy their way into the culture. While the diverse cultures of Mexico and its people are known for their hospitality, there is a fine line between cultural appreciation and appropriation, and the landscape of agave spirits is rife with the latter.

See the reference guide on page 284 to find further reading and resources related to both environmental and cultural sustainability.

How Agave Spirits Are Made

There are five basic steps to making a spirit from the agave plant:

- ▪ Harvesting
- ▪ Cooking
- ▪ Milling
- ▪ Fermentation
- ▪ Distillation

HARVESTING

There are no machines capable of harvesting agaves (yet), which means each and every plant is harvested by hand. The process may be drastically different, depending on whether the agaves are cultivated or wild. Neatly planted rows in cultivated fields are easier to manage than wild-growing agaves that sparsely populate steep mountainsides and sometimes grow directly off the side of rock cliffs. Either before or after the plant is pried from its roots and separated from the ground, a sharp circular blade on the end of a long pole, called a *coa*, is used to cut off the leaves, or *pencas*, leaving just the heart of the agave. Depending on the region and house style, more or less of the base of the pencas will be left on the heart and ultimately impact acidity and flavors in the resulting spirit. The people who do this intense labor are known as *jimadores* or *magueyeros*. Once harvested, the agave hearts, or piñas, are transported by donkey or truck to a production facility.

COOKING

The word *mezcal* comes from Nahuatl words *metl* and *ixca*, meaning "cooked agave." During the cooking process the starches are converted into fermentable sugars, resulting in a sweet and edible product that is still enjoyed today as a treat and can be found in traditional markets throughout Mexico. There are four basic styles of ovens, or *hornos*, used to cook agaves: traditional in-ground ovens, *mampostería*, autoclaves, and diffusers.

Traditional Hornos

The original method of cooking agaves for mezcal is in an in-ground conical pit, oftentimes lined with stones. Local rocks from rivers or streams, or volcanic rock from the landscape, depending on the region, are placed in the pit along with local wood, and a fire is lit. Once the stones are red-hot, the piñas are layered into the oven, cushioned with fibers from the last production in between the hot coals and raw piñas so as not to char them. Once filled up, the oven pit is covered with straw mats, tarps, or sheets of metal and then covered with earth. Sometimes a little water is added inside to encourage steam, but not always. This is the step that can impart a smokiness to some agave spirits. The piñas are cooked for two to four days, or sometimes longer.

*Previous: Jimadores, or agave farmers, in Jalisco, Mexico, harvest blue agaves used to produce ArteNOM tequila. **Opposite:** Preheating the horno at Sacro Imperio in Nombre de Dios, Durango, is a 12-hour process.*

Horno de Mampostería

Made from bricks, concrete, clay, or other fireproof materials, masonry ovens are traditional in tequila and raicilla production. These ovens are typically heated from below or above and use steam to cook the agave hearts. This process usually takes a full day, with some variation in timing; generally speaking, a slower cooking process is associated with artisanal quality.

Autoclaves

Autoclaves are a German technology and function like large pressure cookers. They are efficient and can be finessed and customized for longer or slower cook times and higher or lower pressure settings. While there is some controversy within the industry about the use of autoclaves in artisanal tequila, in blind tastings autoclave cooking was not found to have a great effect on the final flavor when compared to other steps in the process, such as fermentation.

Diffusers

These machines use a chemical solution to strip raw agaves of their starches and convert them into fermentable sugars. Since this does not actually cook the agaves, I do not technically consider these types of agave spirits mezcal or tequila (tequila falling under the umbrella of mezcal). The process yields a flavor that is bereft of the natural sweetness and pungent flavors that traditionally made agave spirits have. This technology is widely used, but most brands do so secretly, going to lengths to not disclose their use of diffusers in the process—adding even more reason to be skeptical of this technology.

MILLING

Once cooked and cooled, the piñas need to be crushed to release the juice within the fibers. There are three main ways to mill: by hand, with a millstone or *tahona*, or using a machine.

Milling by Hand

The oldest way of doing this, still practiced today, is to crush the piñas by hand with large wooden mallets. Sometimes the agaves are chopped into small pieces with a machete and then pounded. A small depression or hole in the ground may be used for pounding, or sometimes a hollowed-out tree trunk is used as a container in which the piñas are crushed.

The team at Lalocura hand milling roasted agave to prepare for fermentation at Palenque la Candelaria, where Lalocura mezcal is produced.

Use of Tahona

We can see the influence of technology brought by Europeans in what is still considered artisanal production with the use of a *tahona*, or large stone wheel, that is drawn around a pit by a donkey, horse, or mule. In some cases, the animal has been replaced by a machine, slowly pulling the millstone over the cooked piñas until they break down into juicy pulp.

Milling Machines

Milling machines or shredders are common all over agave-producing regions. While at first thought this may seem much less romantic for traditional spirits, it also eliminates backbreaking work that is usually not fairly compensated.

FERMENTATION

This is where the magic happens. The elements that go into fermentation have consistently accounted for the most variations in final flavor among blind tasters. There are many variations to consider when it comes to fermentation, including how the crushing method will affect it.

Fermenting with or without Fibers

Traditionally, mezcal is made by fermenting the juicy pulp including the fibers; however, many tequilas ferment only the juice from the cooked and crushed piñas without the fibers. Fermenting with fibers typically leads to more complex flavors. If using fibers in fermentation, the more even the crush is, the more consistent the fermentation will be. This is neither inherently good nor bad, but it will have an impact on the final flavor. Hand-crushing produces the most varied sizes and pieces of agave pulp, whereas machine-crushing will produce a consistent crush throughout. An uneven fermentation is more likely to produce a wider range of flavors, which could lead to more complexity or result in disjointed flavors. Like many other steps in making spirits across the globe, the higher the risk, the higher the potential reward.

Use of Cultivated or Natural Yeasts

For mezcal, it is traditional to rely on wild ambient yeasts to induce spontaneous fermentation. For tequila, on the other hand, it is most common to use a proprietary cultivated strain of yeast—often considered the crown jewels of a company, and sometimes highly guarded behind locked doors like a bank safe. Using cultivated yeast ensures a more consistent flavor profile and poses less risk of something going wrong during this crucial step of the process. In some regions, a percentage of *pulque* the fermented aguamiel of agave, is added to kick off fermentation with its own live yeast colonies.

Fermenting with or without Water

Whether or not water is added to the fermentation tanks depends on many factors, including tradition, water source, and climate. Some areas add a little warm water to get the temperature right to start fermentation. Other times water is added to boost volume. Sometimes it is added to varieties that are particularly dry. The water source is important, and many old distilleries were built near sources of water, some standing today as relics and monuments of ancient distilleries.

Containers

All kinds of materials can be used as fermentation containers: animal hides and pits carved into stone, aboveground wooden and stainless-steel tanks, concrete and wood-lined in-ground tanks, and even large plastic containers.

Duration

The time it takes fermentation to complete is widely varied and heavily dependent on the climate of a region. An average time is four to seven days, although some cooler areas report fermentation times up to three weeks.

DISTILLATION

Distillation is the process of separating out the alcohol from the other compounds, mainly water, of a fermented mash. All stills use the same principle of applying heat to the mash. Alcohol turns into a gas at a lower temperature than water, allowing it to rise and pass through a system of tubes submerged in cold water until condensing back into a liquid. This final alchemical process of distilling the fermented cooked agave mash into a spirit encompasses many variations, including the materials, the number of distillations, and the style of still.

Distillation is a hands-on process for artisanal mezcal. There is typically a sleeping mat or sometimes even a mattress in the distillation area, because once it starts, it does not stop until it is completed, which can span more than one day and night. Most stills are powered by wood fire and tended to by human hands that manage the heat masterfully, based on experience. The heat of the fire will dictate how fast, slow, and smooth the distillation process is. Concurrently, the master distiller will taste, smell, and visually assess the *perlas* (bubbles) of the distillate to make cuts of heads and tails. Heads and tails are the first and last parts of distillate to come out of the still, with the center part known as the heart. The heart offers the most balance of alcohol and organoleptic qualities (the elements you can taste and smell) and will be the base of the final product. Heads and tails, along with distilled water, may be blended into the heart to achieve the desired alcohol level before final bottling.

A traditional wood-and-copper still that uses internal condensation for La Luna Mezcal in Michoacán.

Still Materials

Like other elements of production, the materials used will vary depending on tradition and region. The most common materials used are copper, steel, clay, wood, and carrizo, a bamboo-like plant. In some regions it is common to see repurposed materials joined together with ingenuity to create a functioning still. Copper and steel are the most commonly used materials, and they do not impart their own flavor to the final product. It's worth noting that copper attracts sulfur compounds that form during all fermentation processes, so in addition to being an excellent conductor it also serves to remove those undesirable flavors. Steel doesn't have this same effect but is a much sturdier material. Wood and clay can both impart and absorb flavors during distillation. For example, mezcals made using stills that have a significant wooden element may be less smoky than others, and mezcals made using clay stills often have a creamy mineral overtone that the clay imparts. Similar to aging wine in oak, these flavors are not good or bad, simply part of traditions and enjoyed, or not, based on one's subjective preferences.

Clay and repurposed plants like hollowed-out tree trunks, agave leaves, carrizo, and spent agave fibers are considered to be ancestral materials. It is also common to see a mix of metal and nonmetal materials in some regions, particularly metal and wood in regions north of Oaxaca. It is worth noting that in all of the distilling equipment there tends to be at least one piece of copper, like the copper pans for condensation in wood and clay setups.

Distilling with or without Fibers

Mezcal is always distilled with fibers for the first fermentation. For tequila, regardless of whether fermentation was with or without fibers, the fibers may or may not be included in the first distillation. As with fermentation, the inclusion of fibers leads to more complexity in the final flavor while also requiring a specific skill set to masterfully distill with the additional material.

Number of Distillations

All mezcals, including tequila, are distilled at least twice; it is after this second distillation that the products become Mezcal. The one semi-exception to this is a refrescadera still, which employs a cooling and plate technology that allows the spirit to be something like 1.5 times distilled within one distillation run (see the description of refrescadera on page 35 for more details). Many tequilas are triple-distilled to create smoother and silkier flavor profiles, though this can sometimes strip the final spirit of flavor compounds if not done masterfully. Some mezcals are distilled more than twice, either because it is made from a variety that requires additional distillations to be palatable or to include flavor enhancing and/or medicinal ingredients in a subsequent distillation.

Still Shape & Style

Most artisanal mezcal is produced in small stills, while the size of stills for tequila production varies widely. The two most common styles of stills used for agave spirits are pot stills and column stills. Additionally, Filipino-style internal condenser stills are common in mezcal production, as are uniquely engineered stills where materials and resources are scarce.

Tequila is comparable to other spirits categories, mostly using traditional column or pot stills, but mezcal has as many still variations as there are distillers of mezcal. The tradition of making mezcal is intertwined with a tradition of resilience, innovation, and unique engineering, often with repurposed materials.

Pot Still

This is the most common still used for all spirits for most of history. Typically, it is metal-based and made up of a potbelly-shaped mash chamber that is heated from below and a bell-shaped top with a metal tube that exits the top through which the vapor passes; the tube gently slopes down and forms a coil, which is surrounded by cool water. In this coil the vapor cools down and condenses back into a liquid and drips out of a spout as a distilled spirit.

Filipino-Style Stills with Internal Condensation

These types of stills are often called Filipino style, crediting this distillation technology to Filipino people, who have a tradition of distilling coconuts.

Wooden Hat Still

This type of still uses a metal mash chamber, fueled by fire underneath, and an upper chamber made out of wood, with a metal (usually copper) condenser set on top of the wooden hat that holds cold water. The distilled vapor condenses into liquid internally, where there is a plate, spoon, or other collector that transfers the liquid to a spout, out of which comes the distillate.

Clay Still

In a clay still, two clay pots sit on top of one another. The bottom clay pot is fire-heated from below. The top clay pot is bottomless, allowing the vapor to pass up into it, and the top of the upper clay pot has a plate (sometimes metal, sometimes other materials) through which cool water flows, condensing the liquid on the underside of that plate on the inside of the upper clay pot. Inside there is a plate or spoon, often made out of an agave penca, carrizo, or other natural material, that transfers the liquid to a spout, out of which comes the distillate.

Column Still

A column still passes the vapor through a series of perforated plates, through which increasingly pure vaporized alcohol passes as the impurities fall back down. These types of stills can be calibrated for a customized result. The taller the column and the more plates in the still, the purer the result. This style of still is efficient and continuous, and it eliminates a lot of the work involved with labor-intensive pot stills, which require manual operation for each distillation and cleaning between distillation runs.

Refrescadera

Traditionally found in the Miahuatlán and Ejutla regions of Oaxaca, this unique style of distillation carries out an accelerated refinement in just one pass. The refrescadera is a cylindrical piece encapsulating the *capitel*, or bell-shaped hat of the still, forming a chamber. It is filled continuously with cold water, which forces the rising vapors to condense into liquid and fall back down into the mash chamber, and they will have to work extra hard to get back up and through to the serpentine. It is this process that refines and etches out a higher proof and purer distillate. The vapors that make their way through the cooler temperatures of the refrescadera apparatus will then enter the serpentine in the external condenser and exit as mezcal. Distillation is the refining process, and while distillation with refrescadera reaches high alcohol levels, similar to a second distillation, it doesn't do the same amount of overall refining as a second distillation would. The vapor passing through this extra step is what makes it like one and a half distillations in one. Oftentimes, this process produces spirits that do not pass the chemical limit tests for official certification, although they are in no way dangerous to drink, and usually very delicious.

The first distillation at the Siete Leguas distillery; the *ordinario* is always distilled in copper and with fibers.

Above: Clay stills at Fabrica El Sabino in Santiago Matatlán, Oaxaca. **Below:** Stills at the palenque of Ignacio "Don Chucho" Parada in Santa María Zoquitlán, Oaxaca, used to produce releases for Nuestra Soledad and El Jolgorio.

Mezcal

DENOMINATION OF ORIGIN

A denomination of origin (DO) is a system that certifies products and goods based on many factors, including where, how, and from what something is made. DOs seek to protect and denote traditional products or ingredients, certifying that they are typical of or in line with a certain heritage. A well-known example is Champagne, which can only be called Champagne if the wine's provenance and production follows the strict rules of the Champagne DO; otherwise, it is sparkling wine.

It is important to note that while quality is often conflated with having a DO status, the DO is intended to inform consumers that a product follows traditional methods but does not guarantee quality; there are plenty of non-DO status sparkling wines that are better than certain Champagnes. The organization responsible for the denomination of origin system in Mexico, the Mexican Institute of Industrial Property (IMPI), recognizes that DOs are not created; rather, they are assigned to an existing culture or tradition to protect and certify its authenticity, but not necessarily its quality.

There are eighteen DO protected goods from Mexico. Six are for spirits, and four of those are for agave spirits.

AGAVE SPIRIT DOS

DO	YEAR FOUNDED
Tequila	1974
Mezcal	1994
Bacanora	2002
Raicilla	2019

For many years mezcal was seen as a kind of crude moonshine. In the early 1990s, a group of Oaxacan producers and community members organized to advocate for an official DO certification to distinguish between real mezcal and improperly produced spirits, some of which were causing illness and death and jeopardizing the reputation of the spirit.

The history of colonization, repression, and mass extermination of Indigenous people, plus the fact that Oaxaca is one of the poorest states within Mexico, are other factors that have contributed to bad actors taking advantage of and exploiting producers whose need to make money to feed their families supersedes all else. As a living, evolving culture, it is no surprise that it is a work in progress to come up with and apply regulations that adequately describe—let alone protect—all that mezcal is. And many in the industry argue that the current Mezcal DO is not sufficient.

The Mezcal DO began as a literal copy of the Tequila DO, with the word *mezcal* replacing the word *tequila* throughout the legal document. This is problematic for a few reasons, not least of which because Tequila is historically and culturally one niche subvariety of the broader mezcal category, and the production processes and traditions are vastly different. There have been corrections and attempts to rework the DO, but it can still feel like trying to shove a square peg through a round hole. In some cases, the regulations (like chemical limits of acidity) actually cause producers to change their typical production processes in order to pass the standards of the DO—which accomplishes the opposite of what a DO is designed to do.

I think of the umbrella category of mezcal—meaning all agave spirits—similar to the way I think about Italian wine, which has hundreds of subregions and individual DOs, each of which denotes the specific traditions of that place. Without the hundreds of DOs, we wouldn't be able to identify or appreciate the distinct beauty of Chianti, Barolo, and Etna as easily—it would all just be Italian wine. Similarly, we have a massive category of Mezcal with no formal distinctions, when there is an opportunity to appreciate Minas, Sola de Vega, and Etucuaro, and so on as regions with their own terroir.

DESTILADO DE AGAVE

What happens if a producer refuses to change their traditional recipe to fit the (sometimes arbitrary) standards of the DO? Or if they can't afford the process? Or perhaps they want to take a political stand against the DO and/or organizations that certify. Any spirits that, for whatever reason, choose not to be certified as Mezcal are known as *destilados de agave*, or agave distillates. Culturally they are mezcal, but legally they are prohibited from using the word on their labels. As a practical matter, exported destilados are sold, bought, and listed alongside Mezcal on menus and shelves. Within Mexico, however, it would be wise to pay extra attention to the provenance of any uncertified spirit, for the sake of authenticity and to avoid consuming something that may be adulterated or dangerous. While the highly curated exports are not targets for adulteration, there is still a local culture of selling adulterated or less than 100% agave "mezcal" to unsuspecting or uninformed buyers. Because the vast majority of the spirits included in this book are exported or otherwise verifiable, I do not specifically distinguish between certified or uncertified mezcal.

UNDERSTANDING DO

Mezcal DO

The Mezcal DO is constantly changing, shifting, and evolving. Please check the sources listed in the resources guide (page 284) for the most up-to-date information. This represents the most current and relevant information for consumers as of writing this at the end of 2021.

REGIONS

In order to be certified, a spirit must be made from 100% agave and come from one of ten states of Mexico:

- Oaxaca
- Guerrero
- Puebla
- Michoacán
- Guanajuato
- San Luis Potosí
- Tamaulipas
- Zacatecas
- Durango
- Sinaloa

It is both legally allowed and traditional to use agave that is not local and is purchased from other areas or other states. This serves to highlight the hand of the maker and native yeast aspects of mezcal terroir, since the listed origin of a mezcal may reflect where it is made, not necessarily where the agave comes from.

MEZCAL'S CURRENT APPELLATION
aka "Denomination of Origin," or "DO"

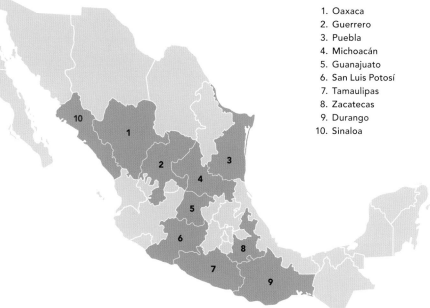

1. Oaxaca
2. Guerrero
3. Puebla
4. Michoacán
5. Guanajuato
6. San Luis Potosí
7. Tamaulipas
8. Zacatecas
9. Durango
10. Sinaloa

CLASSIFICATIONS

In addition to being certified as Mezcal, the spirits may be classified as "artisanal" or "ancestral." Unfortunately, poor regulations make these labels mostly useless. For example, artisanal mezcal can still contain industrially produced products and use industrial manufacturing processes. Similarly, the parameters of what can be considered ancestral are too strict and sometimes exclude spirits that are produced using methods that are considered ancestral by the larger agave spirits community.

In this book I use a commonsense approach to the terms, not necessarily the legally defined terms:

■ Industrial: Mezcal produced in large batches, often from underripe agave. Use of nontraditional technology such as autoclaves or diffusers. (Legally, this type of mezcal can be called mezcal.)

■ Artisanal: Handmade using traditional methods in small batches from ripe, seasonal agaves by people who are part of the culture. (Legally, if

the bottle says "artisanal," it will not be made using an autoclave
or diffuser.)

- ◼ Ancestral: Production practices from before the technology introduced
  by Europeans, such as the *tahona* and metal pot stills—hand crushing,
  materials like clay, animal hides, hollowed-out tree trunks, carved stone
  tanks, carrizo, and internal condensers as in the Filipino style of distillation
  (see page 34).

It's worth noting that most mezcal, other than Tequila, is not aged in wood.
The age of the spirit correlates with the age of the plants at the time of harvest
and/or any additional glass aging. The best mezcals express the flavors of the
plants, something that wood can cover up or interfere with, so wood aging is
usually reserved for batches of mezcal that are not considered top tier or prized
expressions. Some wood-aged mezcals are still made to honor a patriarch or
matriarch of a producer family who developed a taste for it a few decades ago
when it was fashionable. Those tend to be very tasty. Other wood-aged mezcals
are made to appeal to whisky drinkers and don't leave much room for the agave.

AGING & INFUSION STATEMENTS

These categories describe the different flavor-enhancing processes that agave
spirits go through before bottling, such as wood and glass aging, infusions, or
additions during distillation.

- ◼ Joven: no significant wood aging
- ◼ Reposado: wood aged less than one year
- ◼ Añejo: wood aged more than one year
- ◼ Descansado en vidrio: aged in glass
- ◼ Abocado con: infused post-distillation; examples include herbs
  or a worm
- ◼ Pechuga: This style of mezcal is made by placing ingredients
  (traditionally seasonal fruits, nuts, and spices along with a piece of or
  whole animal) either directly in the mash, or suspended above it, for
  the third or final distillation. The added ingredients impart their own
  flavor. *Pechuga*, which means heart or breast, is a style of mezcal that is
  traditionally made for and shared during special occasions like weddings,
  births, funerals, and parties.

Tequila

Similar to the Mezcal DO section, this is a recap of the most relevant information for consumers and is not a complete description of the Tequila DO; please see the reference guide (page 284) for resources to find the most complete and up-to-date information.

AGAVE VARIETY

Tequila must be made exclusively from Tequilana Weber Azul, or the blue agave variety. There are many species of agave endemic to Jalisco and the other regions protected under the DO; however, they are excluded from the DO. Blue agave is speculated to be a variety of *Agave angustifolia*, which would make it genetically similar to espadín, the most common variety used to make mezcal.

REGIONS

The vast majority of tequila is produced in Jalisco, but legally it can be produced in 180 municipalities across five states:

- Jalisco (entire state)
- Michoacán (thirty municipalities)
- Nayarit (eight municipalities)
- Guanajuato (seven municipalities)
- Tamaulipas (eleven municipalities)

BASE MATERIAL

While tequila is traditionally and historically an agave-based spirit, the DO only requires that a spirit be made from 51% agave and allows for up to 49% spirit that is made from other base materials; this type of tequila is called *mixto*. All bottles of certified tequila will either say "100% agave" or "mixto" on the label. This style was popularized during a time when producers needed to stretch their production volume, and it snowballed into a massive category that is cheaper and easier to produce. Even though mixto is legally permitted and a popular style throughout Mexico and the world, it is not in line with the tradition or origins of tequila; therefore, I have not included anything other than 100% agave-based spirits in this book. I am hopeful that one day the legal terminology may be amended to reflect the rich heritage of tequila as a 100% agave-based spirit.

ADDITIVES

Four different types of additives are legally allowed in tequila, as long as they make up less than 1% of the liquid. The additive categories are glycerin (which provides an oily, full mouthfeel), caramel color, sugar syrups, and oak extract. While it is easy to understand why a company may add a minuscule amount of caramel color to get a consistent appearance across different batches of an añejo tequila, for example, there are many tequila companies that use this legal allowance to define their flavor profile. This is a shame. Happily, the independent organization Tequila Matchmaker (page 286) has begun unofficially certifying brands as additive-free, giving customers insight into which brands may be using color-, texture-, and flavor-changing additives.

AGE STATEMENTS

- Blanco/plata/silver: No significant wood aging
- Joven/gold/oro: A blend of blanco and reposado or añejo
- Reposado: Aged 2–12 months in oak barrels
- Añejo: Aged 12–36 months in oak barrels that do not exceed 600-liters capacity
- Extra añejo: Aged at least 36 months in oak barrels that do not exceed 600-liters capacity
- Cristalino: Aged tequilas that have been filtered to become clear in appearance

Other Agave Spirits

Agave spirits are produced all over Mexico, with hundreds of regionally specific traditions. There are three other DO-protected spirits that are sibling categories to tequila, in that they are specific subvarieties under the historical category of mezcal. In this book, raicilla, bacanora, and sotol are included in the mezcal entries, lists, and directories.

RAICILLA

Raicilla is a regional spirit from sixteen municipalities of Jalisco and one municipality of Nayarit. The production follows the same basic principles of artisanal mezcal. The two subregions are the coast (*costa*) and the mountains (*sierra*).

BACANORA

Bacanora is a regional spirit from thirty-five municipalities of Sonora. The spirit faced one of the strictest prohibition eras, which formally ended only in the 1990s. The culture of clandestine production created a tradition of uniquely engineered stills often made using repurposed and upcycled materials. All bacanora is made from the pacifica agave variety, an *angustifolia*.

SOTOL

Not technically agave, sotol is a spirit that is produced and consumed like other agave spirits made from the dasylirion plant, also known as desert spoon and sotol. Sotol is produced in Durango, Coahuila, and Chihuahua. The family of plants is similar to agave but does have key differences, including having male and female plants, and the ability to produce more than one quiote, or flowering stalk, in its lifetime. The flavors skew vegetal and tart. Interestingly, sotol-inspired spirits are produced in the United States from locally grown plants, most notably in Texas and California.

How to Read a Label

Information on the label of a bottle of agave spirits can be grouped into one of two categories: information that provides insight into the prospective flavor or heritage of what's inside, and information that may be interesting for a variety of different reasons, such as holograms that certify the authenticity of certified mezcal. There are also other key differences between tequila and non-tequila agave spirits. I will focus on the information that is most likely to inform flavor, style, and quality.

- **Alcohol content**
- **Producer/brand**
- **Batch number**
- **Region**
- **Variety**
- **Age statement**
- **Infusions or other flavorings**

MEZCAL LABELS

Since the mezcal category is much larger than tequila, the labels tend to have more detailed information of the provenance of the spirit within.

Look on the bottle of mezcal for the name of the producer and/or the community. This information is the quickest way to assess the spirit's style, especially since single producers often make mezcal for multiple brands, and single brands often work with multiple producers. It's best to follow producers rather than brands. One of the benefits of buying producer-owned mezcals is that you are automatically following the producer and don't need to double-check who is making a particular batch. See page 291 for a list of producer-owned brands.

Scan the label for any particular DO status, like raicilla, bacanora, or sotol; all of these designations include specific information about varieties, regions, and general styles. Also, check for the variety or varieties of agave being used, which is typically listed prominently on the label.

Next, check the alcohol content and if there are any production notes about infusions, or type of distillation, like clay or ancestral distillation, or any glass aging statements. Batch numbers may be helpful if you are searching for particular lots. While it is interesting to note whether or not a spirit is certified mezcal or destilado de agave, it doesn't end up making a difference or informing flavor or quality.

In short, for mezcal I am scanning the bottle for a producer name, a town or municipality in addition to the state of origin, variety of agave(s), alcohol content, and any production or aging notes. This combination of information will help decipher what kind of spirit it is. Much of this information is not required but often included, and it can serve as a green flag when included or a red flag when omitted—particularly when it comes to the producer name or town. If both of those are absent from the bottle, it's generally not a good sign.

TEQUILA LABELS

Tequila labels are generally much more straightforward, with the brand name and logo front and center.

To start, look for bottles labeled "100% agave." Since tequila can be made from up to 49% other base ingredients, all bottles must disclose whether or not they are made from 100% agave. The next thing to look for is the aging statement: blanco, reposado, añejo, extra añejo, cristalino (see page 44 for the detailed breakdown of these styles). The alcohol content will also be listed on the label, which will almost always be 40%, but may have some variation up to 55%. Other elements like batch numbers and NOMs will also be on the bottle and can provide information for those who like to get geeky.

WHAT IS A NOM?

NOM stands for Norma Oficial Mexicana and is also sometimes referred to as a NORMA. The NOM number that appears on all bottles of tequila indicates that the spirit is in compliance with the standards governed by the Consejo Regulador del Tequila (CRT), the body that oversees and regulates the spirit's production. More importantly to consumers, the NOM number is a way to identify which distillery bottles the tequila. Some distilleries produce multiple brands, and the NOM number makes this easy to identify.

Mezcals also have NOM numbers, but unlike tequila, where the CRT is the single body that oversees the certification, there are currently up to five organizations that can legally certify Mezcal for producers within the DO. The practical value of mezcal NOMs to the consumer is not the same as for tequila.

Mezcal is regulated by NOM-70, which defines the categories and production processes of what can legally be labeled Mezcal once it has been certified. The organizations in charge of certifying DO-protected Mezcal are fraught with politics and a work in progress. Up until the beginning of 2021, there was one organization that certified all products for the mezcal DO. Political turmoil complicates the matter significantly, and there are currently competing organizations and no lack of controversy, all of which makes it even harder for producers to go through the system. While often quite public and dramatic, the politics of who certifies mezcal need not be front of mind when deciding which brand to buy. Fortunately, there are several ways to better understand what is inside a bottle.

Page 286 in the resources guide has a list of websites where you can look up NOMs for agave spirits. The websites provide a wealth of information that's updated regularly.

Tequila & Mezcal Today

Prior to the turn of the twenty-first century, agave spirits were often considered harsh party drinks that needed chasers or accompaniments (looking at you, salt and lime) in order to get them as a shot down one's throat. The public's collective understanding has shifted in the last twenty years in the direction of appreciating both the provenance and wide variety of earthy flavors that occupy this category. (We see this evolution, as well, in the culinary traditions of Mexico with the explosion of Mexican fine dining restaurants around the world.)

As this newfound appreciation for agave-based spirits has expanded, there has been an explosion of interest from celebrities, big-money investors, and major beverage companies in financing and producing new brands. As the interest from consumers outside of Mexico to understand the nuance and regionality of Mexico's native spirits has heightened, tourism to the nation's traditional production areas has substantially grown, enhancing even more the allure of the spiky succulent known as agave.

CELEBRITY BRANDS

Like non-celebrity brands, there is a mix of quality among celebrity-owned and -backed brands. In general, celebrity brands are overpriced and do not represent the best quality or flavor of what is available. Some of the most common issues when it comes to celebrity brands, aside from not tasting great, are a lack of transparency in production and provenance of source material, promoting someone that has no connection to the culture as an authority over the artisans and experts that carry generations of experience, and contributing to a culturally extractive model.

However, some celebrities are genuinely invested in their brands. With the best of intentions, they take the time to get to know the process and people behind their products. In any case, and regardless of intentions, they may not be qualified or able to distinguish refined flavors and textures, resulting in a product that falls flat in comparison with products made by true masters of their craft.

Are celebrity brands necessarily bad? No. But the bottom line is that if you are searching for the best spirit, the best value, or a combination of the two, you are unlikely to find it in the bottle of a celebrity-owned brand. You are much better off seeking out small artisanal producers whose heritage and experienced palates inform what's in the bottle. See the resource guide on page 286 for a list of websites that keep the most up-to-date information about producers and their affiliations.

TERROIR

The mezcal industry borrows the word *terroir* from the wine industry, where it is used to describe the sense of place a product has. The concept of terroir, the literal translation being *earth*, is understood to encompass the region, soil, altitude, variety, yeasts, traditions, and a producer's unique production style—all of the production elements that affect the final product.

A terroir-driven spirit transports you to that place with each sip, just as a certain dish might taste like home. The fact that mezcal is so defined by its terroir is another characteristic that makes it so much more than a mere product; drinking mezcal is a way to connect with a culture and its people and environment.

I believe we need a term that is unique and specific to agave spirits. There are likely terms from the Indigenous languages of agave spirit–producing cultures that would be more appropriate, but for now, we will use terroir.

Tequila Terroir

Focusing on the regions in and around the valley of Tequila, where the vast majority of tequilas are made, there are two distinct subregions: Los Altos (the highlands) and El Valle (the valley). It's worth noting that the valley, sometimes erroneously called the lowlands, sits at nearly four thousand feet above sea level. The two regions have different soil compositions and microclimates, resulting in different sizes, sugar contents, and ripening schedules of the agaves grown in each region. The generalization about flavor is that tequilas made from Los Altos agaves show fruitier and sweeter flavors, while tequilas made from El Valle agaves feature the earthy and peppery characteristics of the plant. As with all generalizations, there is some truth to this; however, as a practical matter, it's not that simple. In reality, most producers source agaves from both regions and mix them together. There is nothing inherently wrong about mixing agaves from the two subregions, though some brands add to the confusion by presenting their products as representative of the region where their distillery is while using agave from a mix of regions in their spirit. The brands that do source exclusively from one of the two subregions typically feature that on their websites or bottles, specifically stating that they use 100% highland or valley agaves.

Even tequilas that are made from 100% regionally specific agaves do not necessarily correspond to the generalized flavor profiles. Some brands include specific information about soil and elevation in order to showcase how these traditional elements of terroir impact a tequila, and at least one brand

(Tequila Ocho; see page 104) uses a system to delineate specific parcels, like single vineyards for wine. Tequila terroir is much more complex than simply noting "valley" or "highlands"; it has more to do with the growing conditions, stage of ripeness, and human aspects of terroir. Some of the most influential human aspects include how close a shave the piñas get during the *jima* (the process of cutting the leaves from the heart), cooking method, yeasts, and fermentation style.

Mezcal Terroir

The intricacies and nuances of mezcal terroir could fill an entire book. The primary aspects to consider are variety and ripeness of agave, region and subregion, production techniques, and hand of the maker. While that list seems concise enough, each of those categories could be elaborated on at length. One of the most interesting aspects of terroir for artisanal mezcal is the exclusive use of natural ambient yeasts, which give each mezcal a specific flavor of its place. One exception to this is when pulque, fermented aguamiel, is added to initiate fermentation—but even in this case, ambient yeasts are being used via the naturally fermented pulque. Like sourdough bakeries, yeast colonies cultivate themselves in fermentation areas and are a big contributor to the particular flavors of any given production facility.

For those interested in diving headfirst into exploring the many facets of mezcal terroir, I suggest tasting many espadín-based mezcals from Oaxaca, ideally from different subregions and made using different techniques. From there, branch out to other states, focusing on the most common agave variety for each region, for example Cenizo from Durango and Cupreata from Michoacán. Keeping the agave variety consistent allows one to perceive the differences in flavor from other elements like still materials and regional traditions. Discovering the many intricacies of mezcal terroir is an ongoing adventure that will continually inspire more questions than answers.

VISITING DISTILLERIES

The town of Tequila is a popular tourist destination. Many of the large tequila houses offer regularly scheduled tours that are easily accessible to English-speaking visitors, including day trips from Guadalajara, Jalisco's capital. The best way to plan your visit is by perusing the options listed on the websites of the distilleries you want to visit. Visiting small or private production facilities often requires a personal connection and invitation. Those looking for a more intimate and educational experience, or access to some of the distilleries off the beaten path, should consider signing up with a private tour company like Experience Agave, whose tours are planned and led by industry insiders with longstanding connections in the region.

Traveling to mezcal-producing regions is decidedly more complicated. In general, mezcal-producing communities are not designed for outside visitors. Recently, some brands have made moves to offer public tours in the style of tequila distilleries, though some common ways people visit producers are by having a connection, by directly messaging a producer family, and increasingly, by booking a tour if the distillery has a website.

The most common place to visit for firsthand mezcal experiences is Oaxaca, specifically the nearby town of Santiago Matatlán, considered the world's capital of mezcal. Visitors can stop in at the many public-facing tasting rooms, called *expendios*, that line the main road of Matatlán, often with their palenques and homes in the back and available to visit.

I do not recommend visiting, or asking to visit, facilities that are not specifically open to the public unless an invitation is extended.

I strongly recommend planning a tour and booking with a local person. The Mezcalistas website offers a comprehensive list of vetted local tour guides and organizations.

Like areas of Oaxaca outside of Matatlán, other mezcal-producing states are mostly accessible through private tours. It is not recommended to venture out on your own, go on spontaneous visits, or search for producers without prior planning and reliable connections.

The foundation of visiting any foreign place is humility. If you are interested in traveling to mezcal-producing regions, I invite you to ask yourself: What impact will my visit have on traditional mezcal-producing communities? It's important to center the well-being of the communities that produce mezcal when considering or planning a visit.

Here are some guidelines for those who decide to visit and wish to do so humbly and respectfully:

- Know your place. You are a guest in another culture. You are not entitled to anything. Accept what is offered graciously.
- Pay the hosts. Many producers don't have tour rates, so how much you pay is subjective and often up to you. If they offer something for sale, purchase something. Tip generously. Even if you don't purchase anything or they have nothing for sale, tipping is a way to show your gratitude for their hospitality.
- Learn some basic Spanish. Oftentimes Spanish is a second language for producers, and even if your guide has assured you it's not necessary, learning some basics is a way to put effort into respecting a foreign culture.
- Bring a gift, something from the market, like fruit, cheese, chocolate, pulque, or a specialty from your hometown.
- Ask questions, ideally in Spanish.
- Be polite. Say hello and goodbye to everyone, without forcing a handshake or other physical interaction.
- Ask before taking pictures or video, especially of people.
- If you think something is priced too low, offer to pay more.
- Tread lightly, and make an effort to adapt to the local customs.
- Bring your gratitude back home. Oaxaca has experienced disproportionate forced migration, and Oaxacan and other Mexican and Indigenous people are all over the United States. They are concentrated in the service industry and continue to offer their hospitality, culture, and knowledge.

How to Enjoy Tequila & Mezcal

SELECTION & COLLECTION

Sometimes there is a batch of distillate that speaks directly to your heart through your taste buds. Buy a couple bottles of that one if you can and put one away to enjoy later. Avoid buying out the entire batch of spirit; it's nice to give others a chance to taste a small batch, as these are one-of-a-kind productions of that particular time and place. Treasure them, but do so respectfully. Collecting

Previous: 100+ year old masonry ovens; agaves enter through the top holes and a fire from wood and dried cactus is made in the "doors" below to cook the piñas.

expressions is a way to honor and relive the moment you first tasted it. Or save it to commemorate a special event.

STORING YOUR SPIRITS

Traditional mezcal will age in glass and has a long shelf life when stored in a cool, dry, and preferably dark place. Storing full bottles is best; the less oxygen in the bottle, the better. To that end, consider transferring partial bottles to new glass containers that don't have extra head room, and remember to label them with all pertinent information. It is not recommended to store spirits in plastic. Lastly, remember to enjoy your collection—mezcal is best enjoyed in *copitas* (tiny cups) among friends and family, not on a basement shelf.

CHAPTER 2

TASTING 101

t's tempting to drink mezcal as a precious elixir, just a few small sips here and there. However, I have found that the sprits are best enjoyed as an experience of conviviality, similar to the way you would share a bottle of wine.

Tasting an agave spirit is a sensual experience. The first step is to fully appreciate the aromas, keeping a small opening in the mouth to encourage a healthy flow in the oral and nasal cavities. I often inhale and exhale multiple times to let the full bouquet unfurl, as I hover the spirit just below my nose. The next step is to take a small sip, as if you were just gently kissing the spirit. Some people like to keep it in their mouth for a few seconds or longer before swallowing and exhaling. The flavors stay pungent on the soft palate and linger in the breath, especially for that first exhale. Flavor-sensing cells are positioned to capture the aroma as you exhale, and this is very much the finale of every sip. Savor it before indulging in any chaser or accompaniment.

TASTING STEP BY STEP

1. Smell the spirit while keeping your mouth slightly open.
2. Inhale and exhale fully a few times.
3. Take a small sip and let the spirit fill your mouth for a few seconds.
4. Swallow and feel the sensations and flavors.
5. Exhale and notice the flavors that travel up the back of the throat.
6. Inhale and exhale a few times before taking another sip.

Previous: Tequila aging barrels at distillery El Llano. **Opposite:** A tequila tasting.

Glassware

Because of the difference in alcohol, flavors, and styles, I recommend different glassware for tequila and mezcal.

GLASSWARE FOR MEZCAL

Because of the high alcohol content of mezcal, it is best served in a wide shallow dish. Traditional serving vessels such as *jicaras* (hollowed-out half gourds), small clay copitas, and hollowed-out animal horns all allow plenty of surface area for alcohol to waft off the top. The most common cup is the *veladora*, a repurposed small glass candle holder that can hold about two ounces of liquid. Prep bowls, teacups, and rocks glasses are all options that work well for serving mezcal.

Some traditional vessels, like jicaras and unglazed clay, will absorb some of the mezcal as they sit, something to keep in mind when pouring rare or limited spirits.

In a bowled glass, like an all-purpose wine glass, which is suitable for most spirits, the alcohol can sometimes pool and collect in the airspace above the liquid and be intense when one goes to take a sip. If I am served in this type of glass, I gently blow into the glass to disperse the surface air and encourage more oxygen so the spirit can breathe. It's worth noting that some people like this concentration of alcohol and actually prefer a snifter or wine glass for their mezcal.

There are also a few ergonomically designed copitas made specifically for mezcal. For me, the best flavors and aromas are coaxed out of mezcal when sipped out of TUYO copitas (page 61), which are handmade from high-quality porcelain. They are shallow and have a small lip, accomplishing the best of both worlds of a wide surface area while keeping the aromas tightly nestled against the top of the liquid's surface. I do all of my mezcal tastings from these copitas, and strongly recommend them to anyone who wants to experience the organoleptic qualities from their mezcal, and other spirits, more fully and deeply.

GLASSWARE FOR TEQUILA

Traditional *caballitos* are tall, narrow shot glasses, but they do not leave much room for appreciating aromas or letting the spirit breathe. I find that wide, shallow glasses like rocks glasses provide plenty of space for aromas to collect without overwhelming the nose with alcohol. All-purpose wine glasses and champagne flutes are other popular options that work well for most tequilas. For tequilas that are 45% or more ABV, I treat them like I would mezcal and use the corresponding glassware.

Serving & Accompaniments

The best way to serve spirits is the way you, or whoever is drinking them, likes best. I like to drink mezcal and tequila the way it is most often appreciated by the people who make it: neat, at room temperature. Serving on the rocks, with a splash of soda, with a citrus twist, or even with a grind of black peppercorns can enhance some spirits, the same ones that are most suited for cocktails (see page 223). Fine mezcals are difficult to improve upon by adding other ingredients, which is why I usually don't.

It is customary to serve snacks alongside agave spirits. All flavors—salty, spicy, fruity, rich, sweet—are welcome. Chapulines, cheese, fruit with salt, *carne seca*, chicharrón, nuts, seeds, and chocolate are all typical botanas. The snacks balance the absorption of the spirit into the body and enhance the flavors by giving them something to bounce off of—like counterpoint in music or adding salt to your chocolate.

Typical Flavors and Aromas

The many different aromas and flavors present in mezcal can be broken up into categories that are familiar to the palate, mainly fruity, sweet, earthy, spicy, smoky, lactic, and umami. Below are some of the most common aromas and flavors to help get you started describing your spirits in detail. If you can't quite put your finger on a specific note, try using the categories themselves to describe the spirit, for example, smoky and spicy, or earthy and sweet.

Above: Tuyo Copitas.

FRUITY	EARTHY	SMOKY
Mango	Grass	Leather
Citrus	Herbs	Hardwood smoke
Pineapple	Pineapple husk	Roasted pineapple
Melon	Asparagus	Smoked chilies
Berries	Mineral	
Banana	Metal	
Flowers	Ink	**LACTIC**
Peach	Pine	Cheese
Squash	Clay	Butter
Cranberry	Roasted coffee	Cream
Cactus fruit		
Guava		

SWEET	SPICY	UMAMI
Chocolate	Green chilies	Sea salt
Caramel	Red chilies	Meat
Vanilla	Dry chilies	Mushroom
Sugar, rock candy	Mace	Funk
Brown sugar, *piloncillo*	Cinnamon	
	Cardamom	
	Paprika	

Organizing a Tasting

You can arrange a tasting for yourself and others to become better acquainted with agave spirits. Here is a quick checklist of elements to help ensure a successful and enjoyable experience.

- Select a reasonable number to try. Agave spirits are potent, so more than four to six spirits total could be overkill for the palate.
- Plan a tasting order. Generally speaking, you should choose an order based on alcohol content, starting with the lowest ABV and working your way to the highest ABV spirit. For every spirit there should also be a snack; even if you don't plan on highlighting food pairings as part of the tasting exercise,

it's important to have snacks that will break up the flavors in the mouth and balance the alcohol as you imbibe. Choose one snack for each spirit.

■ Have plenty of glassware. It's interesting to compare aromas and flavors side by side, ideally in the same type of glassware. One glass per unique spirit is best. For larger tastings, consider investing in sets of glassware, even if they happen to be small pinch bowls or candle holders from a thrift store.

■ Provide plenty of water. This should go without saying, but stay hydrated. This is so important, especially when mixing different distillates

■ Create a theme. This is an optional extra step. Consider grouping spirits by region(s), producer, or variety. Keep it consistent or design a compare and contrast tasting. Another option is to use a food theme to anchor a tasting, such as chocolate or cheese + mezcal.

■ Use a map of Mexico as you taste to understand where each spirit comes from. A good visual representation can help you pinpoint what regions and subregions make the mezcal you enjoy most.

Food Pairings

Agave plays well with food, even more so than other spirits. Especially when it comes to mezcal, the many layers of flavors represent just as many opportunities to create successful pairings. In addition to pairing with snacks, desserts, and/ or main courses, mezcal is often enjoyed as an aperitif and a digestif. While not a true pairing, it does help awaken the appetite and stimulate digestion, each an important aspect of thoroughly enjoying food experiences.

Starting with traditional tried-and-true pairings will educate the palate and allow you to work your way into developing more experimental combinations. Consider the characteristics of traditional pairings:

■ Salt, acid, sweet: salt and fruit

■ Spicy, crunchy: *chapulines* (grasshoppers) and *cacahuates* (peanuts)

■ Lactic and salty: cheese

■ Sweet, roasted, creamy, bitter, astringent: chocolate and coffee

■ Complex and layered: mole

From here, you can add your own ingredients while sticking to the flavor templates of traditional pairings. For example, a rich stew or curry in place of mole, chips instead of chapulines, or some sort of bitter lettuce or greens (such as chicory, endive, or kale) with vinaigrette instead of coffee.

Pairing boards can be a creative way to highlight one or more mezcals as well as experiment with multiple flavor combinations. If you find something you like, you can re-create those flavors in a composed meal. For example, if you love a certain tequila with a particular cheese, then building a meal around peppers stuffed with that cheese and using that tequila in a cocktail will have echoes of that successful pairing.

Try serving a pairing board as a dessert course. As a rule of thumb, anything that would typically pair well with dessert wines, like pungent cheeses drizzled with honey, should also work well with mezcal. Bright, salty cheese like feta and goat cheese are also nice accompaniments. Perhaps counterintuitively, smoky cheeses or items with a smoke element don't make for the most interesting pairings with smoky mezcals and tend to overshadow crisp tequilas; one exception is smoked meats that have substantial sauces or rubs as a featured flavor.

SEASONAL PAIRING BOARDS

When composing a pairing board, I like to mix it up by including some traditional and some nontraditional elements. Below are seasonal pairing boards that follow a similar template and make the most of what's in season in my region. Use these as inspiration, and feature ingredients from your local favorites to make it your own.

PAIRING BOARD CHECKLIST, ONE OR MORE OF EACH

- Cheeses
- Dried fruits/preserves (dates, cherries, fig jam, honey)
- Fresh fruits or vegetables
- Flavored salt (smoked salt, *sal de gusano*)
- Chocolate
- Crunchy salty snack (nuts, seeds, chapulines, chicharrones)
- Crackers, tostadas, bread

Seasonal pairing boards should feature the freshest ingredients while also relying on local and sustainable options. Because seasonal ingredients are at their flavor peak, they offer the most pungent and rewarding pairing potential.

**SPRING
(LA MEDIDA TEPEZTATE)**
Aged Gouda
Mango preserves
Strawberries, figs
Pickled radishes
Beef jerky
Sal de gusano
Flourless chocolate cake
Chicharrónes
Pumpernickel crackers

**SUMMER
[TOSBA TOBALA]**
Garlic herb goat feta and/or washed
  rind cheese
Peach preserves
Sour cherries
Garden vegetables (snap peas, green
  beans, tomato, herbs, etc.)
Fennel salt
Chocolate almond bark
Chapulines
Sourdough

**AUTUMN
(LÁGRIMAS DE DOLORES
MASPARILLO)**
Triple crème bloomy rind cheese and/
  or sharp Cheddar
Roasted honeynut squash compote
Mole and tortillas
Pecans
Concord grapes, pears
Bitter and spicy greens like chicory
  or arugula
Chili salt
Chocolate pumpkin loaf
Toasted pumpkin seeds
Buckwheat crackers

**WINTER
(REAL MINERO ESPADÍN)**
Blue cheese
Honey
Dates
Radishes, apples
Miso caramel
Ginger berry salt
Dark chocolate–covered espresso beans
Roasted mixed nuts
Shortbread

CHAPTER 3
TEQUILA

Anyone serious about tequila knows that selecting the right bottle isn't easy. The sheer number of options available on the market can make it overwhelming to sort through brands, both old and new. However, it is well worth a little digging to find the hidden gems.

Rather than categorizing tequila based on how long it may have been aged in wooden barrels, I like to categorize tequila based on the heritage and current practices of the producer. I see three major categories of brands in the current world of tequila.

- The brand started with the best of intentions by someone from a tequila-making heritage, born from passion and a desire to proudly share Mexican culture . . . and ultimately sold to an international conglomerate for large amounts of money. Too often, these brands turn into studies in marketing and maximizing production and profits, at times at the expense of the environment and the heritage once associated with the brand. The founding story may remain, but not necessarily the substance of what inspired the brand or the quality that made it famous to begin with.

- The brand started by an outsider to quench a personal thirst for something not already on the market. This type of brand assumes that whatever they are making is going to improve the category, for example by changing a flavor profile to suit a different or wider audience or employing some type of experimentation that is not beholden to tradition. These brands can sometimes produce delicious spirits and inspire new trends within the category.

- The brand committed to quality and tradition above all else, most often founded and run by families that have a long legacy in the region and in tequila production. Typically, these brands are not the largest or most recognized outside of the craft tequila industry, but they are usually the most delicious and satisfying, and offer the best quality-to-price ratio.

Previous: An oven at La Vencedora tequila distillery for Siete Leguas in Tequila, Jalisco.
Opposite: De la Purisima church in Main Square, Tequila, Jalisco, Mexico.

No matter which category a brand falls into, the reality is that production methods, flavor profiles, and internal brand philosophies are constantly changing. What is a small craft tequila today could be the next billboard ad brand bought out by a multibillion-dollar conglomerate next year. These entries and tasting notes are a time capsule of the industry at a time of exponential growth, metamorphosis, and perhaps identity crises for tequila. I have tried to include information in an impartial way to help define the landscape of the sea of brands. I leave it up to you, the reader, to draw your own conclusions.

The entries are grouped by brand and listed in alphabetical order. In addition to background information about each brand, the town, state, and NOM are listed. Each individual offering is listed by name, with alcohol by volume, a rating, my general comments, average retail price for US consumers, and a tasting note.

All spirits were tasted in 2021 from then current release bottles with notes and information that reflect the ownership and brand status in 2021.

With each entry, I have provided a price and ratings breakdown.

PRICE	RATING
$ 1–35	1—not recommended
$$ 36–65	2—good
$$$ 66–100	3—great
$$$$ 100+	4—exceptionally delicious
	5—desert island bottle

As always, preferences are subjective. I focus on aroma, flavor, mouthfeel, finish, and overall balance in each spirit. It is entirely possible for my tastes to be out of sync with consumers and other agave spirits professionals. It is my sincere hope that the information herein will serve as a helpful guide for both new and experienced tequila drinkers.

LISTINGS

ARETTE

Tequila, Jalisco, NOM 1109

Owned and operated by the Orendain family, the Arette available today was formally relaunched in 1986. Brothers Eduardo and Jamie are the fifth generation to carry on the family legacy of one of the most recognized families of the region. Arette is made from estate-grown agave at distillery El Llano, the distillery where previous generations of the family started their tequila-making journey in the early 1900s, then revamped in 1978. The tequilas are little known in the United States, though I expect this will likely change as more consumers become familiar with the high quality-to-price ratio their expressions consistently offer.

ARETTE FUERTE 101 BLANCO

ABV: 50.5%
PRICE: $$
RATING: 3.5

A bright and spicy overproof blanco. Use it to take margaritas to the next level. ■ Fruity and gently sweet cotton candy and soursop aromas, with flavors of juicy summer melon, finger limes, and clementine. There is also an herbaceous side that peeks through, with hints of tarragon and pineapple basil. The spice stays nicely centered on the tongue.

ARETTE SUAVE REPOSADO

ABV: 40%
PRICE: $$
RATING: 2.5

The barrel notes are strong but don't overwhelm the cooked agave notes. ■ Sweet baking spice, leather, and butterscotch characterize the nose. The flavors are roasted, with hints of pineapple, baked peach, and hay. Cinnamon and more caramelized sugar flavors surge on the suede-like finish.

ARTENOM

Various, Jalisco, various NOMs

A collaboration between individual producers and agave spirits pioneer Jake Lustig, ArteNOM is unlike any other tequila brand. Rather than having just one distillery, or NOM, the brand is made up of specially selected batches from different distilleries, highlighting the art of each NOM (as the brand name implies). Sourcing from different distilleries makes this brand one of the most terroir-focused lines of tequila. The labels of each bottle prominently feature the NOM associated with it, making it clear that this is a tequila made from the distiller, not for a marketing demographic. What is consistent across each release is a high standard of quality, with a significantly lower price tag than many other brands advertised as "super premium." These are often the bottles I reach for to give as gifts to my friends who know and appreciate great tequila.

1414 REPOSADO

ABV: 40%
PRICE: $$
RATING: 5

An elegantly aged spirit, delicious on its own or paired with dessert and cigars. A very special treat and incredible value. ■ Tropical fruits like dried banana and papaya mix with tapioca pudding, all deliciously inviting aromas. This one starts out soft and custardy, but quickly turns to a suede-like texture, full of cinnamon, cedar, and creamy coffee. The juicy finish is ripe with baking spices and tobacco.

1123 BLANCO HISTÓRICO

ABV: 43%
PRICE: $$
RATING: 4

Made by the Rosales family at the Cascahuín distillery in a vintage style where blanco tequila is rested for less than one month in ex-brandy barrels that previously held Oaxacan mezcal. ■ Light straw color gives away the historical-style production of this gently aged blanco. The aroma is pure cooked agave, supported with notes of pear and apple, and a hint of smoke. The buttery texture hugs the palate, offering flavors of spices, almonds, roasted pineapple, and a star anise finish. Crisp and luxurious.

BIRBÓN

Tequila, Jalisco, NOM 1437

Birbón, meaning "rascal," is a relatively new brand of tequila made for Palm Bay International, importers of some of the most well-known wine and spirits brands on the market. The tequila is made using a combination of traditional pot still distillate as well as column still distillate. The value-driven brand is marketed for cocktails.

BIRBÓN BLANCO

ABV: 40%	A mildly flavored but well-balanced tequila that would work as a base for many cocktails. ■ Baked vanilla custard and freshly cut grass are balanced aromatically. The rich flavor is ripe with minerals, Asian pear, and white pepper. The texture is smooth, and the finish is clean.
PRICE: $	
RATING: 2	

BLUE NECTAR TEQUILA

Amatitán, Jalisco, NOM 1459

Founded in 2010 by Nikhil Bahadur and his father as a passion project, Blue Nectar was acquired by Paradise Brands in 2020. The tequila is produced from 100% blue agave from the valley of Amatitán by brothers Roberto Real Reynoso and Fernando Real Meza at their own distillery, founded in 1998. Before founding their own distillery, the family had decades of experience as agave farmers, and they still use their own agaves for their tequila production. The brand is known for aging in North American ex-whiskey and ex-bourbon barrels, which master blender Guillermo Garcia Lay combines to create the signature smooth and bold wood-aged tequilas. In addition to the aged expressions, Blue Nectar also produces an unaged blanco tequila.

BLUE NECTAR BLANCO

ABV: 40%
PRICE: $$
RATING: 3

Crafted separately from the base spirit for the aged expressions, this is triple-distilled to achieve a velvety texture. ■ Refreshing aromas of pineapple husk, sea salt, and lime zest. Light and buoyant, the flavors in the mouth are earthy and crisp with freshly cut grass followed by salted cucumber, and key limes—all bright and tangy.

BLUE NECTAR REPOSADO EXTRA BLEND

ABV: 40%
PRICE: $$
RATING: 3

An extra-rich reposado that contains 5% extra añejo. Bold enough to enjoy on its own or alongside a cigar, or as a stand-in for whiskey in cocktails. ■ Straw colored in the glass, with aromas of caramel, smoke, and bittersweet chocolate. The silky texture is ripe with deep flavors of vanilla and baking spices, and it has a long oaky finish.

BLUE NECTAR AÑEJO FOUNDER'S BLEND

ABV: 40%
PRICE: $$$
RATING: 3

This tequila is rich thanks to a 5% addition of a five-year aged extra añejo. The deeply wooded notes are to the fore without overpowering the agave core. ■ Rich amber-brown, with equally distinct aromas of pipe tobacco, dried oranges, salted caramel, and vanilla. Full in the mouth with notes of sticky toffee pudding, date loaf, and sweet vanilla at the fore, followed by a bittersweet chocolate finish.

CALLE 23

Arandas, Jalisco, NOM 1545

Sophie Decobecq is the woman behind this consistently delicious and affordable brand. A French woman turned agave distiller, Sophie moved to Mexico in 2003, launching Calle 23 in 2009 as its owner and master distiller. As a biochemist and engineer with a background in cognac, Sophie brings her own twists to production. She isolated three natural yeasts from the agave fields for fermentation, selecting the strain depending on which expression—blanco, reposado, añejo—the final product is destined to be. While not strictly traditional, her hands-on approach, with just a touch of mad scientist vibes, is what makes this brand unique.

CALLE 23 BLANCO

ABV: 40%
PRICE: $$
RATING: 4

One of the best and most value-driven all-purpose blancos available. ■ Refreshing aromas of sweet grass, herbs, and freshly split pineapple waft from the glass. Like the aromas, the flavors are clean and crisp while remaining ethereal and nuanced. Starting soft and gently sweet, steely minerals and peppery vegetation blossom on the midpalate. Spicy and chalky, with some oily viscosity, the finish is pungent, long, and elegant.

CALLE 23 REPOSADO

ABV: 40%
PRICE: $$
RATING: 3

Gently kissed with barrel influence. Even agave purists would enjoy this aged expression. ■ Gentle aromas of brown sugar, coconut, key limes, and lightly smoked chilies swirl together in this barely tan-hued reposado. The richness unfurls on the palate more than in the nose, with underpinnings of salted caramel, guava, and tobacco supporting the spicy agave core. Warm baking spices plus freshly split agave heart notes linger on the finish.

CALLE 23 AÑEJO

ABV: 40%
PRICE: $$
RATING: 3

An agave-forward añejo that would be nice in stirred cocktails paired with anything grilled. ■ Tan-golden in the glass with pretty aromas of sweet orange oil, vanilla musk, and pipe tobacco. In the mouth the flavors are integrated, starting with toasted almond, sea salt, and dried tangerine peel. More layers reveal soft maple candy, green peppercorns, and mace. The agave character is central throughout, playing nicely with the citrusy finish.

CASAMIGOS

Atotonilco El Alto, Jalisco, NOM 1609

This wildly popular celebrity tequila became an instant cult classic upon its release in 2013, backed by high-profile actor George Clooney and nightclub owner Rande Gerber, who is also the husband of Cindy Crawford. The brand was quickly scooped up by mega conglomerate Diageo for nearly a billion dollars, sending a message to celebrities everywhere that starting a tequila brand could be a fun and fast cash grab. After the change in ownership in 2017, the production was moved to Diageo's own facility, and some have noticed a change in flavor to sweeter and more vanilla focused.

CASAMIGOS AÑEJO

ABV: 40%	Not much agave or unadulterated barrel flavor to be found. ■ A deep
PRICE: $$$	golden-brown color in the glass, with comparatively mild aromas of tobacco
RATING: 1	and chocolate. The flavors are sweet, including vanilla, milk chocolate, and
	corn syrup.

CASA DRAGONES

Tequila, Jalisco, NOM 1489

Founder Bertha González Nieves is considered a pioneer in the contemporary tequila world and was the first woman to be given the official title of Maestra Tequilera from an organization supported by the tequila regulatory board. The brand launched in 2009 with a signature *joven*, and has since added an aged and additional unaged offering to the lineup. Casa Dragones is one of only a few brands that celebrates their use of a diffuser, citing it as a sustainable alternative to traditional processes. The tequilas are known for their smooth texture and mild flavors.

CASA DRAGONES BLANCO

ABV: 40%
PRICE: $$$
RATING: 2

A subtly flavored, ultra-smooth tequila. The light flavors blend best in cocktails. ■ Fresh mint mixes with a piquant, earthy aroma of wet hay. The flavors are very subtle with green vegetal notes and after flavors of sal de gusano and wet earth.

CASA NOBLE

Tequila, Jalisco, NOM 1137

Casa Noble's master distiller and co-founder Jose Hermosillo traces his family's heritage as tequila makers back eight generations to the 1700s. It is produced at La Cofradía, one of the most famous distilleries in the region, which has barrel-shaped hotel pods on the property. Although La Cofradía produces over sixty brands of tequila, the vast majority of production is for Casa Noble. The brand was created in the 1990s with the goal of offering a fine sipping tequila, in contrast to the typical shot-and-cocktail pigeonhole that most tequila had fallen into. Details like using certified organic estate-grown agave, triple distilling, and using French oak for aging impart a status of luxury and refinement to the brand. It was also one of the first brands to leverage celebrity involvement, with Carlos Santana becoming a part owner in 2011. In 2014, the massive beverage conglomerate Constellation Brands purchased the brand and the distillery.

CASA NOBLE BLANCO

ABV: 40%
PRICE: $$
RATING: 4

This shows off how flavorful and uniquely layered tequilas can be when made with care. ■ A never-ending flow of heady aromas reveals olive brine, candle wax, nougat, freshly cut grass, and some very seductive funk. The richness is even more powerful on the palate, with concentrated tropical fruit flavors, green chili spice, crisp minerality, and floral undertones. The flavors evolve in the mouth, taking the palate on a journey with each sip.

CASA NOBLE REPOSADO

ABV: 40%
PRICE: $$
RATING: 2

With all of the sweet barrel notes, this would be best suited for dessert cocktails and hot toddies. ■ Light amber in the glass, the aromas skew earthy, with rain on a forest floor, pine needles, rock candy, and some musk. Barrel flavors come through strong with toasted coconut, caramel, and maple mixing with red chili spice and white grapefruit zest. Roasted pineapple flavors are candied on the finish.

CASA NOBLE AÑEJO

ABV: 40%	A complex añejo well suited for sipping or mixing. ■ Cinnamon and
PRICE: $$	other baking spices are soft aromas. The light texture is luscious in the
RATING: 3	mouth, revealing flavors of cedar, clove, red chilies, and toasted coconut.

Some saltiness creates a butterscotch effect that is balanced by woodsy pine and rosemary herbal notes. The finish is warm, with echoes of spice cake.

CASAZUL

Tequila, Jalisco, NOM 1489

Casazul was founded by Bruce Warner around 2010. The tequilas are made using a diffuser. The brand offers four expressions of tequila: silver, reposado, añejo, and extra añejo. The spirits are designed for mixing into cocktails.

CASAZUL SILVER

ABV: 40%	No agave character left in this one, sadly. ■ Vague aromas of mint and
PRICE: $	fruit, with notes of anise. Watery on the palate, with only a hint of herbs and
RATING: 1	dry eucalyptus with a sharp acetone finish.

CASAZUL EXTRA AÑEJO

ABV: 40%	A pretty color, but not much else redeeming here. ■ Weak herbal tea,
PRICE: $$$	dried peppermint, and wet cardboard aromas do not inspire confidence.
RATING: 1	Vague flavors of chamomile and salt float aimlessly amid the watery texture

before finishing sweet.

CASCAHUÍN

El Arenal, Jalisco, NOM 1123

Cascahuín, translating to "mountain of light," is one of the most authentic brands and producers of tequila available, which spans four generations in the industry dating back to 1904. The distillery itself was founded in 1956 and is still family owned and operated with Salvador Rosales Trejo at the helm. Their tequilas are not the most well known but are among the most delicious. The focus is on sourcing the best agaves and using traditional production methods, including brick ovens for cooking and tahona crushing for some expressions. It is a relatively small operation, and it is clear that this is a labor of love for the Rosales family.

CASCAHUÍN BLANCO

ABV: 40%

PRICE: $

RATING: 5

A pleasure to drink, likely one of the best blancos most people will ever taste. ■ A freshly cracked bottle will give off seductive aromas of night-blooming flowers, cucumber, and grapefruit; like a fine wine, nosing it is half the pleasure. It's cooling, lightly sweet, and silken, then deliciously spicy on the tongue. After each mouthwatering sip, the aromas of lemons and earth softly perfume the palate on exhaling.

CIMARRON

Tequila, Jalisco, NOM 1146

Enrique Fonseca is of the fourth generation of a family of agave growers that owns a significant portion of the region's quality agave. He became a distiller after contracts to sell tens of thousands of tons of agave to Cuervo and Sauza went unhonored. Instead of trying to offload the agaves elsewhere, he bought a distillery from Bacardi in the 1980s and traveled to Scotland to learn about distillation and stills to create flavorful tequilas. The distillery, La Tequileña, produces tequila for multiple brands including Fuenteseca (page 97), Don Fulano (page 88), and ArteNOM (page 72). Cimarron is made from blending column and pot still distillates to create a clean, easy-drinking, and value-driven final product.

CIMARRON BLANCO

ABV: 40%
PRICE: $
RATING: 2.5

Crisp and dry, this is an easy choice for all kinds of cocktails. ■ Freshly cut tart green apple, summer grass, black pepper, orange zest, and slatey minerals are refreshing aromas. Light on the palate with a touch of sea salt, more crisp green orchard fruits, and lime zest flavors. A white peppery and red chili spice swells in the mouth, leaving a pleasant tingly finish.

CHINACO

González, Tamaulipas, NOM 1127

Chinaco is the quintessential brand from the northeastern region of Tamaulipas, and it is the only distillery in the region. A series of events led to a surplus of agave grown in the region having no buyer in the 1970s, and Guillermo González, descendant of a powerful landowner in the region and Mexico's secretary of agriculture, lobbied the government to extend the legal geographical boundaries of the denomination of origin to include Tamaulipas. Finding success four years later, he founded Tequilera la Gonzaleña and began the tradition of making tequila outside of the traditional regions. Those interested in the terroir of agave will be happy to know that the majority of the agave used for their tequila production is grown in the region, with just a small percentage coming from Jalisco. Their artisanal production hasn't changed much since the brand's founding in 1977, and it remains family owned and operated.

CHINACO REPOSADO

ABV: 40%
PRICE: $$
RATING: 3

A well-balanced aged tequila with notes of agave and barrel aging. ■ Aromas of sweet cream and grass layered with cooked agave. In the mouth, there are notes of citrus peel, black pepper, minerals, and light caramel. The finish is ripe with vanilla and gentle baking spices.

CLASE AZUL

San Agustín, Jalisco, NOM, 1595

This eye-catching brand is easily recognized by the bottle's signature hourglass shape and hand-painted designs. Every bottle is handcrafted, mostly by women, in a small town whose economy has been significantly improved by the partnership. The brand has also expanded into home goods like mirrors and lamps, so it's no wonder why many people buy this tequila just for the bottle. Owned and operated by founder Arturo Lemeli and co-owner Juan Sanchez, the brand has resisted many tempting offers to sell to larger corporations, including turning down a billion-dollar offer in 2019. The tequilas may seem overpriced when ordered by the glass at a restaurant but are a value when the bottle is taken home to enjoy—plus you get to upcycle the pretty bottle.

CLASE AZUL PLATA

ABV: 40%
PRICE: $$$$
RATING: 2.5

An expensive but solid tequila. ■ Vibrant aromas of peaches and citrus are lively and refreshing. The flavors blossom in the mouth with rounded jicama sweetness, cucumber, and sugar cane juice before turning slightly spicy with serrano. The finish is smooth and easy.

CLASE AZUL REPOSADO

ABV: 40%
PRICE: $$$
RATING: 2.5

Tasty and rich, this would make a great companion to cheese plates and cream-based desserts. ■ Light vanilla aromas are gently sweet but do not overwhelm the spicy and pepper agave heart. Rich flavors are concentrated and full in the mouth, with baking spices, brown sugar, and sweet baked oats. The finish is long and sweet.

CONFIANZA

Arandas, Jalisco, NOM 1414

An artisanally produced tequila, Confianza is made at the Vivanco distillery from organic agaves. Production includes brick oven cooking and roller mill crushing. During fermentation, classical music is played in the distillery, which is said to stimulate the yeasts. The brand, which launched in the international market in 2020, offers blanco and reposado bottlings.

CONFIANZA BLANCO

ABV: 40%
PRICE: $
RATING: 2.5

Well balanced and easy drinking. ■ Aromatically mild, with notes of musk, tarragon, and grapefruit zest. Crisp and cooling as it hits the palate with plenty of sea salt and mineral flavors, and then ripe tropical fruit and vanilla with a spicy finish.

CONFIANZA REPOSADO

ABV: 40%
PRICE: $$
RATING: 2.5

Bright and punchy flavors in this aged tequila. ■ Woodsy aromas are front and center, with supporting notes of cranberry and cedar. Flavors of burnt caramel and berries are almost sherry-like, with plenty of tannin and astringency.

CORAZÓN DE AGAVE

Ojo de Agua de Latillas, Jalisco, NOM 1103

Along with Pueblo Viejo (page 111), Corazón is made at Casa San Matías. In the last three decades, owner Carmen Villarreal has focused on creating sustainable and favorable conditions for both employees and the environment, with public recognition on both fronts. Corazón, the brand, was launched in 2002 and is currently part of the international conglomerate Sazerac, which owns highly regarded whiskey brands like Blanton's, Buffalo Trace, and Pappy Van Winkle. Corazón utilizes its sister brands' coveted whiskey barrels for special aged releases. The base tequila is produced from estate-grown agaves at the family owned and operated San Matías distillery. Across the board, the tequilas are tasty and well priced.

CORAZÓN BLANCO

ABV: 40%
PRICE: $
RATING: 3

A heady tequila that shows off the floral and fruity side of agave. ▪ Aromas are mildly grassy with a touch of acetone. In the mouth, there are notes of sweet baked pineapple, vanilla, coconut, and soursop. The lively acidity of lime zest along with mineral notes continue to blossom on the tongue. The floral aromas reveal jasmine and lilies mixed with pear and cotton.

CORAZÓN REPOSADO

ABV: 40%
PRICE: $
RATING: 2

An easy-drinking reposado that highlights the barrel notes. ▪ Soft, earthy aromas of almonds and barrel. In the mouth, the flavors are similar, with roasted citrus, blanched nuts, and some gently warming baking spices on the finish.

CORAZÓN AÑEJO

ABV: 40%

PRICE: $$

RATING: 2

A spicy aged tequila. ■ Baked stone fruits and vanilla keep the aromas lifted amid the strong barrel influence. In the mouth, the flavors skew dark and robust with tobacco, cocoa powder, and dried peach. The finish is kissed with cinnamon.

CORAZÓN EXPRESIONES ARTISANAL BLANCO

ABV: 40%

PRICE: $$

RATING: 3

A crisp and clean tequila good for sipping neat or mixing into cocktails. ■ Melons, custardy tropical fruits, and freshly sliced cucumber are refreshing aromas. The texture is soft yet chalky, with flavors of earthy herbs, more cucumber, and a hint of rock sugar. Gentle spice mixes with citrus on the long, flavorful finish. Each sip is a cascade of pleasing flavors and aromas that finish clean.

EXPRESIONES CORAZÓN GEORGE T. STAGG AÑEJO

ABV: 40%

PRICE: $$$

RATING: 2.5

A tasty tequila that picks up significant flavor from the barrel but is ultimately not centered around agave. ■ One might be tempted to think there is not much barrel influence by appearance alone. The pungent aromas reveal the opposite, with immediate notes of peach, vanilla, and spice front and center. Robust in flavor with layers of maple sweetness, mace and nutmeg, charred barley, and a hint of salty minerals. Molasses and green peppercorns make for a spicy-sweet finish.

CORRALEJO

Abasolo, Guanajuato, NOM 1368

Hacienda Corralejo was producing tequila as early as 1775 and is often recognized as the first commercially made brand of tequila. Corralejo was relaunched in the mid 1990s when Leonardo Rodriguez Moreno bought the property—located in Guanajuato, just east of Jalisco—and decided to revitalize tequila production there. But not all agaves used in the making of the tequila are sourced from Guanajuato. For this and other reasons, the focus of this brand is less on terroir and more on value. Similar to other value-driven brands, they use a combination of pot and column still distillates in their final product.

CORRALEJO REPOSADO

ABV: 40%
PRICE: $
RATING: 2

A fine tequila that would be nice in cocktails that showcase the spicier side of the spirit. ■ With a rose-gold hue in the glass, the aromas reveal notes of green and black peppercorns, pineapple husk, and nougat. On the palate, it is sweet, with agave nectar and brown sugar. The flavor is thin in the middle and quickly turns to spiciness that is half peppery capsaicin and half alcoholic burn.

CORRALEJO AÑEJO

ABV: 40%
PRICE: $
RATING: 1

Lacking in flavor intensity, this is a soft and supple aged spirit. ■ A deep tan-colored tequila. Aromas are light and barely perceptible, with an essence of minerals and baking spice. Equally muted on the palate are some notes of nutmeg, roasted red pepper, and toasted grains. Not much agave character comes through within the soft and smooth texture.

DAHLIA

Tequila, Jalisco, NOM 1489

Dahlia was created by the people behind El Silencio Mezcal and launched in early 2021. The tequila is made using a diffuser, aged in white oak for around six months, and then filtered to appear clear. The name of the brand pays homage to the national flower of Mexico.

DAHLIA CRISTALINO

ABV: 40%

PRICE: $$

RATING: 1

This is not a good representation of agave spirits. ■ There is nothing in the aroma to indicate agave at all. In the mouth, there are flavors of vanilla, artificial sweeteners, and some barrel char. The texture is viscous and almost syrupy.

DON FULANO

Tequila, Jalisco, NOM 1146

Don Fulano is one of the flagship brands made at La Tequileña distillery, created by Enrique Fonseca (page 81) and Sergio Mendoza in 2002. Together, the two founders represent many generations in the industry and are jointly committed to crafting pure spirits from high-quality agave, natural spring water, and proprietary yeasts. Don Fulano blends small amounts of column still distillate with a majority of pot still distillate to achieve consistency and 100% estate-grown agaves. The aging barrels come from Europe, including some used for wine from Burgundy, Bordeaux, and Portugal. In general, the brand offers a lot of value across the board.

DON FULANO BLANCO

ABV: 40%
PRICE: $$
RATING: 4

Fresh, vibrant, and crisp, this is an ideal blanco for sipping and mixing. ■ Pungent and fresh aromas of green pineapple fronds, freshly cut grass, juicy orange flesh, and minerally lime zest explode from the glass. It is surprisingly soft on the palate given the power of the aroma, and there are flavors of melon, cactus fruit, and chayote. The finish includes a touch of salt and lots of minerality.

DON FULANO BLANCO FUERTE

ABV: 50%
PRICE: $$
RATING: 5

No alcoholic burn, just clean mineral-rich agave flavor here. ■ Minerals, stones, and herbs characterize the aromas, with just a whiff of something floral. Tangy and bright in the mouth, with flavors of kiwi, ground husk cherries, and pears. As the fruitiness subsides, the stony minerals and gentle green chili spice spread out over the palate. The finish is clean, clean, clean.

DON FULANO REPOSADO

ABV: 40%
PRICE: $$
RATING: 3

An elegant reposado with layers of flavor. ■ Light in both color and aromas, the impact comes when you take your first sip. Rich yet elegant flavors of chocolate, dates, and almonds are well integrated. Some tanginess and saltiness add depth to the roasted agave and nutty notes, followed by a long finish kissed with flamed orange peel and cocoa powder.

DON JULIO

Atotonilco El Alto, Jalisco, NOM 1449

Don Julio González began distilling tequila in the 1940s at just seventeen years old. Over the next forty years he would perfect his craft by studying all aspects of tequila making and build his own distillery. Formally launched under the Don Julio name in the mid-1980s, it has now become one of the bestselling and most recognized brands worldwide. In 1999, the company sold 50% of its stake in order to expand, most notably with additional agave plantations. By 2014, the brand was fully owned by mega conglomerate Diageo, a deal that caused controversy.

DON JULIO BLANCO

ABV: 40%	
PRICE: $	
RATING: 1	

Not much agave flavor to be found here. ▪ Vanilla dominates the nose with confected and sweet aromas. In the mouth, the flavor is disjointed with some sour acidity, harsh spice, and indeterminate earthiness. The finish is burnt and sharp.

DON JULIO 1942

ABV: 40%	
PRICE: $$$$	
RATING: 2	

Confected aromas and flavors taste somewhat artificial. ▪ Subtle caramel and rock candy aromas with tart mixed citrus that opens the palate, followed by more caramel, toasted coconut, and smooth toffee. The finish is medium-long with notes of tobacco and smoke.

EL PINTOR

Tequila, Jalisco, NOM 1137

El Pintor entered the market in 2018 as a passion project created by master tequilero Guillermo Barroso. The tequila is made from estate-grown agaves at La Cofradía, one of the largest distilleries, which produces over sixty brands. With just one tequila offering, their flagship spirit is a joven tequila that is made up of blanco blended with ex-bourbon barrel extra añejo and then filtered to remove any color—the same technique used for cristalino tequilas.

EL PINTOR JOVEN

ABV: 41%

PRICE: $$$

RATING: 1.5

Decent aromas, but not much agave flavor, the silky texture may appeal to vodka drinkers. ■ Freshly cut grass and a hint of light caramel are fresh aromas. It is ultra-smooth on the palate, and the viscous and pillowy texture shows some spice, astringency, and herbal notes. The spice lingers on the finish.

EL TESORO

Arandas, Jalisco, NOM 1139

El Tesoro is made at the family owned and operated La Alteña distillery under renowned master distiller Carlos Camarena, where they also produce Tapatio (page 118). The brand is part of the large conglomerate Suntory in the United States. The bottle is topped by a model of a tahona, the traditional massive stone wheel they use at La Alteña to crush the cooked agave. The fermentation is done in open-top tanks with the agave fibers macerating in the aguamiel. Like other brands produced at La Alteña, the tequilas come with an impressive heritage and are generally delicious across the board.

EL TESORO AÑEJO

ABV: 40%
PRICE: $$$
RATING: 3.5

A nice mix of flavors with sweet barrel notes up front and peppery agave on the finish. ■ Soft in color and aromas, warm notes of crème brûlée mix with tropical fruits. The caramelized sweetness hits the palate first, with candied pear, sweetgrass, and yellow fleshed plum. Flavors of baking spice turn into green chili with a musky undertone. On the finish, it's all roasted agave goodness.

EL TESORO EXTRA AÑEJO

ABV: 40%
PRICE: $$$$
RATING: 4

An endlessly flavorful tequila that leaves the mouth warm and spiced. ■ Aromas of cigar box, clove, and freshly split cedar mix with piney and peppery agave notes. The flavors are hay, vanilla, caramel, red Fresno chili, raspberries, and dried mango. Autumn spices are warming, with cinnamon, mace, and nutmeg, alongside a touch of dried pineapple on the finish.

ESPOLÒN

Arandas, Jalisco, NOM 1440

Cirilo Oropeza, Espolòn's master distiller, built his custom distillery in the late 1990s as a culmination project encompassing a lifetime of working in rum, gin, vodka, and tequila distilleries. He was known for customizing various steps of the process, like cutting the agave hearts into quarters to expose more surface area during cooking, playing music for the yeasts during fermentation, and using a combination of both column and pot stills for distillation. In 2009 the brand was purchased by Campari and has become known for their viral marketing campaigns. With the passing of Cirilo in 2020, it remains to be seen if—and how—the brand or tequila may change.

ESPOLÒN BLANCO

ABV: 40%
PRICE: $
RATING: 2.5

A very popular tequila. ▪ Lively mineral aromas mix with floral and herbal notes of bell pepper and lime. The texture is soft with flavors of sea salt, white pepper, cinnamon, and fresh cream.

EXCELLIA

Tequila, Jalisco, NOM 1110

Jean-Sébastien Robicquet, French winemaker and distiller (of Cîroc Vodka fame), collaborated with tequila master distiller Carlos Camarena on this project, which combines high-quality tequila with French maturation methods. Launched in 2011, what makes this line unique in the ever-growing sea of tequila brands is the aging in Grand Cru Sauternes and Cognac casks. The aged spirits are blended to create bottlings that show off the purity of well-made tequila, supported by gentle notes from the casks.

EXCELLIA BLANCO

ABV: 40%
PRICE: $$
RATING: 2.5

Absolutely silken; would contribute a luxurious texture to stirred cocktails. ▪ Vanilla pudding, crushed granite, and fresh clover are all light and inviting aromas. It feels silken in the mouth, and the flavor expands over the palate with guava, pink grapefruit, and river rocks. Integrated acidity keeps the flavors fresh and primes the palate for another sip.

EXCELLIA REPOSADO

ABV: 40%
PRICE: $$
RATING: 2.5

This tequila was produced at a different distillery with NOM 1139, before production was moved to the current distillery, NOM 1110. ▪ Enticing aromas of butter and ripe guavas are rich and sumptuous. On the palate, the flavors are reminiscent of brandy with honeysuckle, white grapes, and pear. The finish is a touch hot but has plenty of flavor, lingering with notes of toasted pastry and candied citrus.

EXCELLIA AÑEJO

ABV: 40%
PRICE: $$$
RATING: 2

This tequila was produced at a different distillery with NOM 1139, before production was moved to the current distillery, NOM 1110. ▪ Bakery treats and chewy caramel come to mind when nosing this tequila. On the palate is a healthy dose of sea salt, which balances out the sweet undertones and highlights the earthy wood notes. Barrel toast is prevalent on the finish.

FORTALEZA

Tequila, Jalisco, NOM 1493

Fortaleza is both new and old in the tequila world. While formally launched in 2005, there are 140 years of experience and four previous generations of tequileros behind the brand. The story starts with Don Cenobio, an important figure in the history of Tequila, who founded a distillery in 1873. There was a small gap in operations from 1976 to 1999, but then Guillermo Erickson Sauza, great-great-grandson of Don Cenobio, resumed production using traditional methods. He uses brick ovens, a tahona, wooden fermentation tanks, and copper pot stills. Fortaleza has a cult following among bartenders for good reason; they are one of a few brands of longstanding heritage that remain committed to traditional production, not only in their marketing materials, but in the distillery as well.

FORTALEZA BLANCO

ABV: 40%
PRICE: $$
RATING: 3.5

A juicy and supple tequila that goes down easy. ■ Limes, tangerines, and cotton make for soft and juicy aromas. A hint of sea salt refreshes the palate immediately upon first sip, with a buttery smooth texture right behind, giving off flavors of ripe melons, pears, and green peppercorns. The finish is kissed with minerals.

FORTALEZA BLANCO STILL STRENGTH

ABV: 46%
PRICE: $$
RATING: 3

A zesty overproof blanco that doesn't overwhelm the palate. ■ Orange zest is a touch floral, almost like Florida water, with eucalyptus and cilantro aromas. In the mouth, the herbs are even stronger, showing rosemary, chervil, and tarragon alongside key lime, green mango, and white pepper. The finish is lightly infused with mineral-rich pink salt.

FORTALEZA REPOSADO WINTER BLEND 2020

ABV: 46%

PRICE: $$$$

RATING: 5

Well worth the splurge if you can find it. Yum. ■ Soft aromas of coconut cream pie, bourbon staves, and maple-glazed cashews are scrumptious. Intensely concentrated on the palate, wave after wave of tastes unfold: sweet maple syrup, mature pine forest, olive brine, and kumquat. Each layer meshes with the next, giving a supremely refined feel with a rich silken texture.

FORTALEZA AÑEJO

ABV: 40%

PRICE: $$$

RATING: 4

A benchmark example of aged tequila. ■ The aromas are fruity, with notes of strawberries that are both sweet and earthy. On the palate, the agave character is loud and pronounced, with notes of roasted pineapple and charred citrus. Salty minerals and toasted wood notes support the rich agave core.

FUENTESECA

Tequila, Jalisco, and Vista Hermosa, Michoacán, NOM 1146

Fuenteseca is the longest-aged tequila currently on the market, distilled and created under the leadership of agave pioneer Enrique Fonseca (page 81), and imported by Haas Brothers. With innovative foresight, Enrique laid tequilas down in barrels for extensive aging, ranging from seven to twenty-one years. There are also vintage unaged releases that feature terroir-specific agaves—one of the perks of owning large swaths of agave plantations. In some of the older bottlings, the barrel tends to eclipse the agave flavors, but they still make for delicious and educational sips. While sometimes difficult and expensive to source, they are a treat to sip.

FUENTESECA BLANCO COSECHA 2018

ABV: 44.8%
PRICE: $$$$
RATING: 5

Made from overripe agave from the most southern region of Michoacán's tequila denomination of origin. A treasure. ■ Pretty aromas of rock candy, plantain, and camote are both earthy-fresh and lightly caramelized. The sweetness unfurls in the mouth, showing vanilla custard, sweet pumpkin, and white grapes. The soft texture matches the ripe flavors and creates an overall impression of luxury and indulgence.

FUENTESECA RESERVA EXTRA AÑEJO 7 AÑOS COSECHA 2010

ABV: 42%
PRICE: $$$$
RATING: 4.5

Exactly what an extra añejo should be. ■ Leatherbound books, smoke, and cigar tobacco are sturdy yet elegant aromas from this rich golden spirit. Ultra-smooth on the palate, with bold flavors of citrus and vanilla caramel, baking spices, freshly split firewood, and dried pine needles. Spicy and sweet cooked agave notes show through, supporting the thick barrel flavors.

FUENTESECA RESERVA EXTRA AÑEJO 15 AÑOS COSECHA 1998

ABV: Unknown
PRICE: $$$$
RATING: 4.5

Extraordinarily balanced and delicious. ■ Aromas are full of musk, light tobacco, and a touch of vanilla. In the mouth, the flavors of bananas Foster, sweet spice, orange peel, and roses are well integrated and balanced. The barrel notes are rich but not heavy on the silky finish.

GRAN CENTENARIO

Tequila, Jalisco, NOM 1122

One of the oldest brands of tequila, Gran Centenario was founded in 1857 by Lazara Gallardo. Today the brand is part of Proximo Spirits, which is owned by the Beckmann family, descendants and owners of namesake brand Jose Cuervo. While not totally mechanized, the production is no longer representative of the artisanal tequilas that were once considered some of the finest in Mexico. One of the remaining aspects of the brand's heritage can be seen in the bottle shape, which features an art deco design.

GRAN CENTENARIO PLATA

ABV: 40%
PRICE: $
RATING: 2

A gently flavored spirit. ■ Aromas are soft and floral with honeysuckle and melon. The flavor is honeyed with a touch of smoke and an herbal finish.

GRAN CENTENARIO AÑEJO

ABV: 40%
PRICE: $
RATING: 1

Not much agave flavor to be found. ■ Wood and caramel dominate the aromas and flavors alike. A lingering black pepper note on the finish vaguely suggests agave.

HERRADURA

Amatitán, Jalisco, NOM 1119

The iconic horseshoe brand has a long history. A working mezcal production facility predates the formal 1870 founding of the hacienda. The brand was family owned and operated for over 125 years and is credited with releasing the first reposado and añejo tequilas in the 1960s and 1970s. When they updated to a modernized production facility, some elements of tradition were traded in, like tahonas for mechanical crushers, and some aspects such as brick/stone ovens and native yeast fermentation are still used today. Herradura briefly switched to diffuser production during an agave shortage from 2001 to 2010, but ultimately stopped. There was some back-and-forth purchasing of shares of the company in the following decades, until it was sold for nearly $800 million to international beverage conglomerate Brown-Forman in 2007. Wondering why the horseshoe is upside down? Those who want good luck must flip the bottle to pour themselves a drink.

HERRADURA LEGEND 2020 AÑEJO

ABV: 40%
PRICE: $$$$
RATING: 2

Easily enjoyable for lovers of richly aged spirits, but there are plenty of other aged tequilas as good or better at a lower price. ■ Aromas show notes of cigar box, cedar, and musk. The flavors are robust, with dried orange peel, candied lemon, smoked salt, and toasted coconut. Plentiful acidity balances the strong barrel flavors, allowing the agave character to peek through the thick curtain of spice at times. The finish is wooded, if a little thin.

HERRADURA ULTRA 2015 CRISTALINO

ABV: 40%
PRICE: $$
RATING: 1

This filtered aged spirit has added agave syrup, but the sweetness intensifies the sourness, making it taste unripe and disjointed. ■ A confusing set of aromas is mottled with pine, mint, and sour ferments, reminiscent of cleaning products. This identity crisis worsens in the mouth—starting sour, like spoiled milk, followed by a dose of brown sugar. Hints of peppery spice and agave-like flavor emerge briefly before the vanilla candy finish.

JOSE CUERVO RESERVA DE LA FAMILIA

Tequila, Jalisco, NOM 1122

Most people know Jose Cuervo as the ubiquitous cheap tequila that is no doubt responsible for more than a few epic hangovers. What many people don't know is that Cuervo's heritage dates back to the dawning of tequila as we know it. The flagship distillery, La Rojeña, is the oldest running tequila distillery in Mexico. It was officially founded in 1812, but the family's occupation of the land dates back to 1758. Today, Cuervo is owned by the Beckmann family, descendants of Don Jose Antonio de Cuervo. While most of the tequila on the shelf is a far cry from the historical libations of yesteryear, the most artisanal spirits from their lineup are the Reserva de la Familia bottlings. These special batches started as just that—private collections exclusively for the family. In 1995, the company began releasing to the public small amounts of these reserve batches, which are produced using ovens and pot stills.

RESERVA DE LA FAMILIA PLATINO

ABV: 40%
PRICE: $$
RATING: 2.5

A solid example of unaged tequila. ■ Aromas of olive brine, vanilla, and freshly cut grass are bright and lively. On the palate is the sharp bite of cayenne spice, followed by sweeter notes of aloe, vanilla, and a mineral finish.

RESERVA DE LA FAMILIA REPOSADO

ABV: 40%
PRICE: $$$
RATING: 2

The woodsy flavor profile is stronger than the agave flavors that may be hiding underneath. ■ Light amber in color, with almost imperceptible aromas of toffee, nuts, and rubbing alcohol. Flavors of pine and cedar mix with coffee and caramel undertones, finishing with a leathery earthiness.

RESERVA DE LA FAMILIA EXTRA AÑEJO

ABV: 40%
PRICE: $$$$
RATING: 2

Charred barrel flavor takes center stage. ■ Pours a dark copper color in the glass; wafts aromas of fragrant vanilla, caramel, and star anise. The flavors are full of rich cocoa and coffee, followed by candied orange peel, baking spices, and burnt sugar.

LA GRITONA

Valle de Guadalupe, Jalisco, NOM 1533

The eye-catching green bottle is the cherry on top of this reposado tequila. Made by Melly Barajas and her team of women, it is the only expression produced by the brand. The signature light profile is thanks to eight months of aging in ex-whiskey barrels that have already been used to age other tequilas—an intentional step to temper the wood and spice flavors and preserve much of the agave freshness. The tequila, like the brand itself, is a refreshing take on contemporary agave spirit.

LA GRITONA REPOSADO

ABV: 40%

PRICE: $

RATING: 2.5

The rich texture makes this an ideal spirit for stirred cocktails. ■ Tropical fruit aromas mix with musk and salty ocean breeze. Soft and buttery on the palate, the caramel pudding flavor is not too sweet. There are notes of red chili spice and a rich oiliness that coats the mouth. A touch of smoke and sweet tobacco round out the finish.

LUNAZUL

Tequila, Jalisco, NOM 1513

Lunazul was founded by Francisco Beckmann, a seventh-generation descendant of Jose Cuervo, in the early 2000s. It is distributed by Heaven Hill, the American whiskey company. The artisanal tequilas have done well in blind competitions over the last decade, with some inconsistencies from year to year.

LUNAZUL BLANCO

ABV: 40%
PRICE: $
RATING: 2

Smooth and easy. ■ Pungent aromas are filled with white pepper and tropical fruits. The oily texture is full of savory vegetal flavors like thyme and pea shoots, balanced with citrus flavors. A hint of clay-like minerality rounds out the finish.

LUNAZUL REPOSADO

ABV: 40%
PRICE: $
RATING: 2

A sweet reposado. ■ Chocolatey and caramel aromas are decidedly sweet. The flavors are also sweet—brown sugar, burnt sugar, and pie crust. The finish has a hint of bitterness, which balances out the sweetness.

LUNAZUL EXTRA AÑEJO

ABV: 40%
PRICE: $$
RATING: 3

Aged in bourbon casks, this tequila has a lot of barrel flavors. ■ Rich aromas of cola, caramel, cinnamon, and dried orange peel, while flavors of tropical fruit, vanilla, and woodsy cedar fill the mouth. The barrel notes are strong, but the agave core still comes through.

MILAGRO

Tepatitlán de Morelos, Jalisco, NOM 1559

In 1998, two college friends from the United States founded Milagro after tasting a lot of unimpressive tequila while on a vacation in Mexico. Along with master distiller Pedro Juarez, they sought to create a product that retained the sophistication of tradition while adapting to modern technology. They use a combination of pot and column still distillation to maintain efficiency without sacrificing quality. Milagro was acquired by William Grant & Sons in 2006.

MILAGRO SILVER

ABV: 40%
PRICE: $
RATING: 2.5

A good tequila for basic drinks and sips. ▪ Vanilla aromas are soft and sweet. An oily texture gives extra weight to the body, featuring flavors of rounded marshmallow, spicy green chili, and a tangerine finish.

MILAGRO SELECT BARREL RESERVE SILVER

ABV: 40%
PRICE: $$
RATING: 3

A pleasant option for smooth sipping or mixing. ▪ Freshly cut grass, sunflowers, and a whisper of vanilla make for balanced aromas. It is spiced in the mouth, with undertones of kiwi, honeydew, yellow bell pepper, and banana peel. The finish is rich and a touch caramelized.

MILAGRO SELECT BARREL RESERVE REPOSADO

ABV: 40%
PRICE: $$
RATING: 1.5

A little mild in character for a reserve bottling. ▪ Mild aromas of dried pineapple, hay, and honeysuckle open up when swirled. The palate expands with mixed dried citrus, vanilla, and tobacco leaf. The white pepper spice has just a touch of harshness behind it but rounds out with notes of maple and dried herbs. The finish is reminiscent of old-fashioned potpourri.

MILAGRO SELECT BARREL RESERVE AÑEJO

ABV: 40%
PRICE: $$
RATING: 2

A gentle but tasty aged tequila that retains agave character. ■ Dried fruit aromas are clean and tangy from this shiny amber-colored spirit. In the mouth there are more dried orchard fruits, salted butter, hay, and grainy leather. Roasted pineapple husk, minerals, and dried papaya are smooth rather than spiced.

OCHO

Arandas, Jalisco, NOM 1474

This project is a partnership, launched in 2008, between distiller Carlos Camarena and European tequila ambassador Tomas Estes, both heavy hitters in the tequila world. The brand is terroir focused, with detailed descriptions of the provenance of the estate-grown agaves in each batch, including date of planting, harvest, elevation, and sugar content. The ex-American whiskey barrels that are relatively neutral, which make for lightly colored, agave-forward aged expressions. Conceived by and for agave geeks, it is one of the most consistently delicious brands on the market—and at affordable prices, to boot.

OCHO BLANCO 2020 LA LOMA

ABV: 40%
PRICE: $$
RATING: 3.5

Crisp, refreshing, and full of pure agave character. ■ Delicate aromas reveal apples, pears, woody herbs like rosemary and thyme, rock candy, and rich minerals. Refreshing and round on the palate with sea salt, green plantain, white pepper, and pure agave flavor. A crisp, snappy finish, along with vanilla custard and eucalyptus tingle.

OCHO BLANCO 2021 EL PASTIZAL

ABV: 40%
PRICE: $$
RATING: 4

A blanco that has impressive nuance and elegance that pairs with fish or fruit courses. ■ An ethereal, floral aroma of vanilla musk, along with green mango, brown sugar, and red apple blossom. The texture is soft with a chalky mineral overtone. The flavors are equally fruity, with more orchard fruits, black pepper, and a touch of brine. The finish is crisp like autumn leaves and freshly split pineapple.

OCHO REPOSADO 2018 EL BAJÍO

ABV: 40%
PRICE: $$
RATING: 5

Agave-forward with complex layers, it's everything one could ever want from a reposado. Absolutely delicious. ■ The aromas are clear agave, supported by smoked poblano chili, leather, and sweet pipe tobacco. Similarly on the palate, notes of peppery green chili and a rough suede-like texture highlight the grassy and subtle pineapple husk flavors. A veil of vanilla and toffee provides sweet aromas, adding another layer of depth to this tantalizingly complex, light reposado.

OCHO REPOSADO 2021 EL PASTIZAL

ABV: 40%
PRICE: $$
RATING: 3

Made from the first-ever agaves planted on a previous pasture for cattle, it is grassy and punchy. ■ This light reposado is full of tart fruit aromas, showing pomegranate molasses, grapefruit, musk, and smoked green peppercorn. Bursting with freshness, the palate is washed over with pineapple, citrus zest, black pepper, and mineral-rich clay. The long finish is zesty and spicy.

OCHO AÑEJO 2018 LAS PRESAS

ABV: 40%
PRICE: $$
RATING: 4.5

A unicorn in the tequila world these days—an añejo that still tastes like agave. ■ Aromas of cigar box, tobacco, and leather show a more rustic barrel influence, highlighting the peppery nature of ripe agave. Sea salt, dried herbs, cedar, and roasted nut flavors are rich on the palate, with baked pineapple on the mid-palate. Each sip evolves into a smooth cascade of cinnamon, clove, and caramel on the finish.

OCHO EXTRA AÑEJO 2015 LA LATILLA

ABV: 40%
PRICE: $$$$
RATING: 3

A smooth and warm toned aged spirit with plenty of vitality and freshness. ■ The appearance is the only light thing about this extra añejo. The bold aromas encompass roasted nuts, berry preserves, dulce de calabaza, and sweet miso paste. Tons of vibrancy in the mouth, shifting from sea salt caramel to cigar box and baking spice warmth. The gentle warmth mixes with brown sugar, candied citrus peel, and charred rosemary.

PARTIDA

Tequila, Jalisco, NOM 1502

Partida was founded in 2005 yet feels like a classic that has been part of the category for much longer. The brand was named for Enrique Partida, a third-generation agave farmer, and has been in the care of master distiller and blender Jose Valdez since its inception. Partida is an example of thoughtfully combining old-world tradition with contemporary technology. Some unique choices that distinguish the brand from its peers are sourcing only valley-grown agaves, cooking them low and slow in an autoclave within twenty-four hours of harvest, and a fermentation technique that includes native yeasts and a proprietary method of contact with cooked agave solids. With a robust aging program, they source their barrels directly from Kentucky and Tennessee distilleries and fill them within ten days of being emptied.

PARTIDA BLANCO

ABV: 40%
PRICE: $$
RATING: 4

A delicious blanco full of agave character; sip as an introduction to quality tequila, or mix into your favorite cocktails. ■ Aromas of tender green herbs, ripe pineapple, kiwi, and flinty minerals. It hits the palate softly, with a cloud-like texture that is full of peppery spice exciting every part of the tongue. Minerality shines through in the mouth, with green fruit sweetness taking a backseat, leaving the mouth feeling clean and energized.

PARTIDA REPOSADO

ABV: 40%
PRICE: $$
RATING: 4.5

One of the best reposados for the price, hands down. ■ Pouring light gold in the glass with unmistakable aromas of cooked agave, cinnamon, caramel, and creamy coffee notes. Smooth and silky on the palate, the flavors of toffee and sweet tobacco uplift the grassy and roasted pineapple characteristics. Charred vanilla bean, maple, and toasted almonds round out the mildly spicy finish.

PARTIDA AÑEJO

ABV: 40%
PRICE: $$
RATING: 5

Outstanding all around, and an incredible value. ■ Dried fruits like figs, raisins, blackberries, and plums are both ripe and tart. Maple-drenched toasted coconut, crème brûlée, and baked stone fruit are indulgently smooth in the mouth. The sweetness gives way to roasted nuts, charred pineapple, and freshly wet elote leaves, with a cinnamon and tobacco finish.

PARTIDA ROBLE FINO REPOSADO SHERRY OAK FINISH

ABV: 43%
PRICE: $$$$
RATING: 3

This tequila is aged six months in ex-bourbon barrels before being finished for two months in ex–single malt sherry seasoned casks. ■ Soft aromas of vanilla and light maple and undertones of raisins and date syrup arise from the sherry cask aging. In the mouth, it is saltier than expected, but also buttery and caramelized. The texture is lusciously smooth, providing a mouthwatering contrast to the cinnamon spiciness left on the palate.

PARTIDA ROBLE FINO REPOSADO CRISTALINO SHERRY OAK FINISH

ABV: 40%
PRICE: $$$$
RATING: 2

This double-aged tequila is filtered to remove the color. ■ One might mistake this for an unaged spirit upon first smell. But once it hits the palate the aging becomes apparent; notes of freshly cut grass and sea salt quickly turn to maple, caramel, and toasted nuts. The finish is spiced, leaving a pleasant blanket of mild cayenne-like heat on the palate.

PARTIDA ROBLE FINO AÑEJO SHERRY OAK FINISH

ABV: 45%
PRICE: $$$$
RATING: 4

This tequila is aged eighteen months in ex-bourbon barrels before finished for five months in ex–single malt sherry seasoned casks. ■ The aromas skew sweet with underlying complexity of dark chocolate, dried figs, and sticky toffee pudding. The richness hits the palate immediately, with roasted tobacco leaf, dark caramel, and dried pineapple. A hint of salt and some bitterness add dimension to the layers of roasted agave sweetness that linger on the warm finish.

PASOTE

Jesús María, Jalisco, NOM 1579

This brand carries with it generations of tequila makers that are the legacy of the Camarena family. Pasote is made by Felipe Camarena, often referred to as a mad scientist distiller due to his innovations in his custom distillery, influenced by his background in engineering. One example of his ingenuity in the distillery is a built-in system to capture rainwater, reducing his reliance on the spring for his production. Despite his personalized machines and methods, production is completely artisanal and uses estate-grown agaves. Launched in 2016, it's a relative newcomer to the scene, and a refreshing one at that!

PASOTE BLANCO

ABV: 40%
PRICE: $$
RATING: 3.5

A full-bodied tequila bursting with ripe garden flavors. ■ Aromas of pine, eucalyptus, and caramelized pineapple core are bright and inviting. The flavors are equally rich, filling the mouth with notes of grass, sweet basil, sugar snap peas, and cilantro. After a veritable garden of flavors, the finish is crisp and spicy-sweet with a buttery texture.

PASOTE REPOSADO

ABV: 40%

PRICE: $$

RATING: 3

A tangy and high-toned reposado with lots of bright agave character. ■ Herbal and spicy aromas mix, giving an impression of grilled meat with herbs alongside charred pineapple and roasted red chili. The flavors are bright and grassy, with notes of dried and fresh citrus, tart cherry, and silky vanilla. The finish is characterized by sunbaked earth, yellow flowers, and spicy mace.

PASOTE AÑEJO

ABV: 40%

PRICE: $$

RATING: 3.5

A luxurious and indulgent añejo, with all of the freshness of mature agave tequila; would be nice alongside flan or a cigar. ■ Aromas come off smoky, before revealing melon, minerals, and white grapes. It is rich and round in the mouth, with concentrated flavors of roasted agave bathed in vanilla, caramel, and piquant baking spices. The gentle spice is elegant as it persists on the tongue while the mouth stays perfumed with sweet barrel notes on the finish.

PASOTE EXTRA AÑEJO

ABV: 40%

PRICE: $$$$

RATING: 3

A citrusy and woodsy tequila, would be nice paired with flourless chocolate cake or other bittersweet desserts. ■ Tropical fruit aromas of papaya and kiwi are soft, atop sturdy notes of burnt brown sugar and freshly split wood. The spicy wood notes are to the fore in the mouth, showing toasted coconut, roasted tobacco, dried Valencia orange peel, and candied lemon zest. The finish is citrus-heavy with hints of white and green peppercorns.

PATRÓN

Atotonilco El Alto, Jalisco, NOM 1492

Patrón is perhaps the most famous premium tequila brand on the market, thanks to strategic advertising as a pop culture icon. Originally produced by Siete Leguas (page 114), Patrón was created in 1998 by billionaire investors who saw an opportunity for high-end tequila in the US market. By 2002, the company broke out on its own, including relocating to a large warehouse that houses rows of small copper pot stills. In 2018, Bacardi bought Patrón for over $5 billion. While the elements of traditional tequila production are technically in place, it's only their ultra-premium Roca line that can compete in flavor with other artisanal small-batch tequilas.

PATRÓN BLANCO

ABV: 40%
PRICE: $$
RATING: 2.5

Good flavor up front, but falls off on the finish. Overall, a solid product. ■ Subtle aromas of melon and grass are earthy and fresh. The texture is silky smooth with mild flavors of minerals, grapefruit zest, butter, and green cactus fruit. An easy-drinking tequila.

ROCA PATRÓN BLANCO

ABV: 42%
PRICE: $$$
RATING: 3

A fresh and well-made tequila for sipping or mixing. ■ Earthy and sweet aromas of cooked agave, vanilla malt, and freshly cut grass. In the mouth, the flavors are round and sweet with heavy cream, white chocolate, lemon zest, and minerals.

PUEBLO VIEJO

Ojo de Agua de Latillas, Jalisco, NOM 1103

Made at Casa San Matías, a distillery with roots in the tequila industry for over 120 years, this is one of tequila's best-kept secrets. One of the most popular brands in the wells of craft cocktail bars across the country, the spirits are clean and well made. The blanco, in particular, is well suited to mixing and is consistently one of the best values to be found.

PUEBLO VIEJO BLANCO

ABV: 40%
PRICE: $
RATING: 3

A great value. ▪ Bright citrus, grass, and high-toned minerals are crisp and clean aromatically. Equally refreshing on the palate, with flavors of lime zest, roasted pineapple, and tender green herbs. The finish is almost toasty in its richness.

SIEMBRA AZUL

Arandas, Jalisco, NOM 1414

Siembra Azul is owned by one of the godparents of the craft agave spirit industry, David Suro, and produced at the well-respected Feliciano Vivanco y Asociados distillery under master distiller Sergio Cruz. The brand is a master class in transparency and education, featuring extensive production notes on each bottle. The tequilas, produced traditionally with a few modern technological touches, are consistently delicious and well priced. While it may take some hunting, their extended aged and limited-release bottlings are some of the best expressions available.

SIEMBRA AZUL BLANCO

ABV: 40%
PRICE: $$
RATING: 3

A classic and easy-drinking tequila. ■ Steely aromas of minerals and lime have a soft vanilla sugar background. The light candied aromas are balanced by notes of almond, stones, and herbs. The spice is mild, adding to the soft, almost fluffy texture.

SIEMBRA VALLES

El Arenal, Jalisco, NOM 1123

Produced at the Rosales family owned and operated Cascahuín distillery, Siembra Valles is one of the brands from David Suro, a pioneer in bringing high-quality agave spirits to the United States. One of the main aspects of production is not separating out the agave fibers, or *bagaso*, in the fermentation, resulting in complex flavors that are a throwback to the traditional styles of tequila. The most unique product from the brand is the Ancestral bottling. It's a recreation of a historically lost expression from when tequila production was similar to mezcal and was, in fact, called Vino de Mezcal de Tequila.

SIEMBRA VALLES ANCESTRAL LOT 2

ABV: 50.2%
PRICE: $$$$
RATING: 4

This is tequila made like it was two hundred years ago, including post-distillation glass aging. A delicious sip of history. ■ Fire-roasted tomato, smoked orange peel, and red berries are tart and crisp aromas. In the mouth, a gentle smokiness mixes with flavors of spearmint, white chocolate, and minerals. The silky smooth texture binds everything together seamlessly, finishing on a sweet green note reminiscent of pears and cactus fruit.

SIETE LEGUAS

Atotonilco El Alto, Jalisco, NOM 1120

Siete Leguas has been family owned and operated since it was founded in 1952 by Ignacio Gonzalez Vargas. Now overseen by master distiller Arturo Valle-Salcedo, production takes place in a facility that is technically split into two distilleries on opposite sides of the same street. The final product is blended by taste (rather than formula) from the spirits produced at each distillery. The techniques from each location vary slightly, but consistent throughout production are the use of estate-grown highland agaves, fermentation with natural ambient yeasts (both with and without fibers), and careful distillation in small copper pot stills. This house exclusively produced Patrón (page 110) from 1988 to 2002. The joint venture ended, largely due to Siete Leguas's refusal to rush or overcommit to production numbers necessary to satiate growing demand, despite seductive investment offers. Their tequilas are always crowd favorites and offer some of the best quality and value to be had.

SIETE LEGUAS BLANCO

ABV: 40%
PRICE: $$
RATING: 4

A refreshing and classic tequila with elegant aromas that continue to evolve with each sip; would be stellar paired with sushi. ■ Soft aromas of cotton, nopal, and kiwi, followed by fresh and buoyant flavors of mixed citrus, minerals, chayote, and pea shoots. On the supremely smooth finish, there are notes of roses and clay that leave the palate perfumed and primed for the next sip.

SIETE LEGUAS REPOSADO

ABV: 40%
PRICE: $$
RATING: 5

A magical tequila that elevates any cocktail and is always a crowd favorite when sipped neat. An all-around winner. ■ The aromas are subtle, revealing notes of cinnamon, green plantain, citrus zest, and raw pumpkin seeds. A hint of caramel opens on the palate, followed by rich yet delicate flavors of *dulce de calabaza*, leather, dried apricot, star anise, and a hint of coffee. The mildly spicy agave is supported by soft barrel notes, striking an impressive balance.

SIETE LEGUAS AÑEJO

ABV: 40%
PRICE: $$
RATING: 4

Gentle barrel notes allow the agave character while delivering caramelized, nutty complexity. ■ Aromas are gentle. In the mouth, it comes to life, giving flavors of piloncillo and molasses, fire-roasted poblano, pecans, maple sugar, and a touch of smoked leather. Baked pineapple and earthy herbs keep the focus centered on agave, while the barrel notes expand ever outward.

SOLENTO

Amatitán, Jalisco, NOM 1480

Founded by surf filmmaker Taylor Steele in 2019, this brand is inspired by and meant to inspire others to slow down to enjoy the pleasures of life; the name can be translated as "slow sun." It is produced from certified organic estate-grown agaves in a traditional method by Eladio Montes and has a unique rectangular and stripe textured bottle.

SOLENTO REPOSADO

ABV: 40%
PRICE: $$$
RATING: 3.5

A rich reposado that you can sink your teeth into, bold enough to stand up to rich sauces and sweet desserts. ■ Vanilla and caramel are the first aromas, followed by roasted pineapple and woodsy spice. Pillowy and sweet in the mouth, the body is full and ripe with mango, flan, and pastry cream. Mild yet palpable serrano chili spice adds flavor and textural contrast to the otherwise juicy sweet notes.

STORYWOOD

Tequila, Jalisco, NOM 1137

In 2016, chef Michael Ballantyne, Scottish born and Texas raised, was visiting his mom in San Miguel de Allende and connected with master distiller Luis Trejo. Trejo heads up La Cofradía, a distillery that produces over sixty tequilas, the most well known being Casa Noble. Their combined passions for experimentation and cask-aged spirits led to the first tequilas fully aged in single malt Scotch whisky barrels. While the exact provenance of the barrels is secret, we know the hand-selected barrels come from the Speyside region.

STORYWOOD SPEYSIDE 7 REPOSADO

ABV: 40%
PRICE: $$
RATING: 5

Aged for seven months in Speyside casks, this may be the holy grail for those who love both tequila and Scotch. ■ Aromas are delicate with vanilla and caramel atop grassy undertones. Well balanced in texture, it is both soft and round, full of roasted pineapple agave core. The toasted marshmallow sweetness pulls back to reveal toasted grains and butterscotch that come from the Scotch-infused barrel. If this tequila were a piece of music, it would be a symphony. Absolutely delicious.

STORYWOOD SPEYSIDE 14 AÑEJO

ABV: 40%
PRICE: $$
RATING: 2.5

After fourteen months in Speyside barrels, this nervy añejo would do well alongside salty yet delicate dishes, like seafood à la plancha. ■ It pours a soft amber in the glass, with aromas of honey, sweet breakfast porridge, and light molasses. Toasted oats, dried orange zest, and spicy chilies are front and center on the palate, with a slightly leathery texture. The mineral-driven finish has notes of lemon and pomelo with a touch of dried hibiscus.

TANTEO

Juanacatlán, Jalisco, NOM 1551

In 2006 a shift in the laws marked the first time infused tequilas were legally permitted into the tequila category. Four years later in 2010, this bartender- and cocktail-focused brand hit the market. Featuring chili infusions of jalapeño, habanero, and chipotle, the idea was to provide consistently high-quality naturally infused tequilas for spicy cocktails. They also produce a high-ABV blanco, appeasing the agave purists. The company is operated as a co-op that includes eighty-five families and prioritizes hiring women from the community, particularly widows and single mothers.

TANTEO BLANCO

ABV: 42.5%
PRICE: $$
RATING: 3

A straightforward blanco that would pair well with grilled meat and taste great in salsas and marinades. ■ Nicely complex aromas that include melon, grassy meadow, and sweet cooked agave with slightly smoky and fatty notes. The flavor is round and well balanced, with plenty of bright, grassy agave notes. The profile is thick with spice that is persistent but not too hot. A long warm finish is minerally and sugar kissed.

TANTEO JALAPEÑO

ABV: 40%
PRICE: $$
RATING: 3

Highly aromatic with just the right level of heat, this makes spicy margaritas easy and consistent. ■ Nosing this tequila feels like being inside a jalapeño—the spicy seeds, earthy flesh, and astringent pith are right there. The flavor starts with notes of fresh chili before the lively jalapeño spiciness sets in, along with grassy agave and pine.

TAPATIO

Arandas, Jalisco, NOM 1139

Felipe Camarena came from a family of tequila makers whose distillery of the 1800s was destroyed and abandoned during the Mexican revolution. After dedicating himself to growing and selling agaves, Felipe founded La Alteña distillery in 1937 to resume the family tradition of making tequila. His grandson Carlos Camarena is now at the reins, distilling both tequilas made at the distillery: Tapatio and El Tesoro (page 92), earning a reputation as one of the best master distillers today. Between the hand of the maker, estate-grown agaves, and fermentation with a strain of yeast cultivated over eighty years ago, the resulting tequilas are delicious.

TAPATIO BLANCO

ABV: 40%
PRICE: $$
RATING: 5

Full of flavor and character, this is the kind of tequila that makes it too easy to keep sipping. ■ Scrumptious aromas of wildflowers, freshly cut succulents, green pineapple husk, and tropical fruit. The texture is buttery soft in the mouth, revealing gentle punctuations of spice. Pine, berries, a hint of vanilla, mango, and custard apple are peppery with sweet aromas. Beguiling in the way that it continues to unfold, layer by layer.

TAPATIO BLANCO 110

ABV: 55%
PRICE: $$
RATING: 3.5

A dream come true for those who like a little extra punch in their cocktails; try this in your favorite recipes for maximum agave flavor. ■ Clay, mineral-rich soil, green bell peppers, and a hint of citrus aromas are earthy. The flavor is punchy on the palate, bursting with fruity ripeness of mango, green cactus fruit, sea salt, and plenty of delicate spiciness. High-toned flavors seem to dance on the palate, with the earthy aromas providing structure throughout.

TAPATIO REPOSADO

ABV: 40%	
PRICE: $$	
RATING: 2.5	

Thoughtfully aged to bring out barrel notes that complement the natural agave character. ■ Aromas showcase light notes of vanilla and maple sugar, though the core remains agave-forward with peppery agave and earthy pineapple husk. Silken in texture and soft on the edges, warm notes of nutmeg and mace complement dried orange and thyme. A hint of leather on the finish is a nice touch.

TEREMANA

Jesús María, Jalisco, NOM 1613

Dwayne "The Rock" Johnson is behind this brand that was launched in 2020. The tequila is produced in partnership with a Mexican family owned facility that only produces Teremana. Johnson has been vocal about getting to know the people and process behind the product, with a focus on sustainability efforts like composting by-products and a water treatment system for the heads and tails that do not end up in the bottle.

TEREMANA BLANCO

ABV: 40%	
PRICE: $	
RATING: 2	

Clean flavors with a short finish. ■ Soft aromas of vanilla marshmallow and tender green herbs, along with punchy flavors of rock candy, basil, oregano, and pea shoots. There is a touch of peppery spice and green bell pepper finish.

TEREMANA AÑEJO

ABV: 40%	
PRICE: $$	
RATING: 2	

Some agave character manages to show through the thick vanilla veneer. ■ The aromas are agave forward, with a touch of caramel and wood notes from the barrel. The sweet and spicy barrel influence comes through on the palate with brown sugar and an intense vanilla caramel finish.

1800

Tequila, Jalisco, NOM 1122

Originally known as Cuervo 1800, this brand was launched in the 1970s as a sipping tequila. Their lineup, while promoted as ultra-premium, is at least partially composed of diffuser-made tequila. In lieu of winning people over with taste alone, the brand has turned to celebrity endorsements as well as sports team sponsorships. The brand is produced in the same facility as Jose Cuervo and is also owned by the Beckmann family, who trace their roots in tequila back twelve generations.

1800 MILENIO EXTRA AÑEJO

ABV: 40%

PRICE: $$$$

RATING: 1

A hallmark diffuser tequila, the tastiness from the aging in the barrel isn't enough to cover up the uncooked agave flavors. ■ With its beautiful, tanned leather color, it is visually elegant. The aromas are full of dried grapefruit peel, clove, and fresh orange zest, all against a backdrop of woodsy spice. The texture is silky on the palate, with bursts of salted caramel and green peppery agave notes. The flavors fall off quickly, leaving a mild blanket of spice and an aftertaste of unripe, uncooked agave.

21 SEEDS

Tequila, Jalisco, NOM 1438

A newcomer to the growing world of flavored tequila that hit the market in 2019. The brand was built around the experimentations of Kat Hantas, who made a hobby of creating home-infused tequilas and sharing them with friends. The base spirit is produced at Casa Maestri, a distillery that makes tequila for over 140 brands. It is then infused with natural ingredients. These flavor profiles are designed for those who want unique ingredients for specialty cocktails or a full-flavored, yet softer, style of tequila.

21 SEEDS CUCUMBER JALAPEÑO

ABV: 35%

PRICE: $$

RATING: 3

The flavors are rich and concentrated, without any trace of artificial additions. ■ It is clear in the glass, and the aromas are spot on, as if smelling a bowl of freshly cut cucumber and split jalapeños. The soft texture is rich as it coats the mouth, as a gentle spiciness unfurls over the palate, supported by a hint of cotton-candy sweetness. The spice lingers on the palate, leaving behind whiffs of cucumber and peppers just picked from a summer garden.

21 SEEDS VALENCIA ORANGE

ABV: 35%

PRICE: $$

RATING: 3

With layers of orange flavor, it is balanced enough to sip straight or mix into drinks. ■ Richly scented with sweet orange blossom, flesh, and rind, this clear tequila is perfumed with orange throughout. In the mouth, the flavor doubles down on the essence of orange, and the texture is lush. A hint of spice and zestiness on the finish round out the flavors.

21 SEEDS GRAPEFRUIT HIBISCUS

ABV: 35%

PRICE: $$

RATING: 2

A citrus-scented tequila that would work in cocktails. ■ Hibiscus gives this tequila a rose gold tint. The aromas are ripe with mixed citrus: ruby red grapefruit, tangerines, and limes. In the mouth, the citrus zest flavors are echoed, with a soft white pepper spice. Some saltiness and earthiness turns tangy on the finish.

CHAPTER 4

MEZCAL

T here was a time, not that many years ago, when I was familiar with every brand of mezcal available in the US market. But these days, with the exponential growth of the category and explosion of brands over the past three years, I discover new brands almost daily. As interest in mezcal as a product grows, it seems everyone is clamoring to release their own brand as quickly as possible. This has flooded the market, making it even more difficult to navigate the shelves and menus.

I recognize that it is inherently strange for anyone, much less a white American woman, to judge mezcal. Mezcal, unlike other spirits, is often an intimate artistic expression of a family or community. The house style and production process of mezcal often involves traditions passed down through generations and ceremonial aspects, sometimes with religious and/or spiritual iconography involved, like altars in the distillery or crosses crowning the ovens. While we often list one name as the master mezcalero, it is usually a whole family effort, resulting in a product that has the seal of the family built into it.

Given the vastness of the mezcal tradition, there are flavors and techniques that are hyperlocal and unfamiliar to even the most experienced spirits tasters. For these reasons, I chose not to include my personal ratings for mezcal. Instead, I rely on the description of the flavors, textures, and characteristics of the spirit to convey the essence and my perception of the quality of each individual spirit.

The entries are categorized by brand in alphabetical order, with background information for each one. Individual spirits are listed with the information I believe to be most relevant, including producer, town and state, agave variety by common and scientific name where applicable, alcohol by volume, my general comments, average retail price for US consumers, and a tasting note.

Previous: Ancestral wooden stills in Michoacán used to produce La Luna Mezcal, illustrating the expansion of the mezcal-producing sector across Mexico. **Opposite:** *Bagazo*, or dried agave pulp, left over from a first distillation at La Luna distillery in Michoacán.

Where information is missing, it is because it is not available or unverifiable. Some entries will also include a batch or lot number. Artisanal mezcal is batch-specific, though my advice is not to obsess over batch numbers or individual batches; that energy is best channeled into following and supporting producers that consistently release batches you enjoy. Some producers are listed by family rather than an individual in accordance with the customs and preferences of the producer and/or brand. It is important to note that even when one person is listed, there is always a team of people involved in production, especially for midsize and large brands. The person listed as the maestro may be the overseer of others who are doing the hands-on work.

The brands included in this list were chosen based on availability and regional representation, and to showcase trends in the industry. The omission of any particular brand is in no way a comment on its quality or validity.

All tastings were done in 2021 using current releases and their then current prices, with the exception of bottles from my personal collection.

The price breakdowns are according to the following parameters:

PRICE

n/a not yet available or bottles from my personal collection
$ 1–35
$$ 36–65
$$$ 66–100
$$$$ 100+

I hope that this list of spirits is valuable in your journey to discover and appreciate all that mezcal has to offer.

LISTINGS

ALIPÚS

Founded just before the turn of the millennium, Alipús was created by the Los Danzantes/ Los Nahuales (page 179) team as a way to feature and recognize the local mezcal traditions of different Oaxacan villages. The brand showcases the aspects of terroir from varied subregions and also provides an economic lifeline to the producers as more consumers inside and outside of Mexico develop a passion for craft mezcal. Karina Abad oversees the operations for the brand, working closely with the producing families. Alipús was one of the first brands to focus on traditional terroir-driven bottlings for export, making its way into cocktails and becoming one of the first mezcals to intrigue bartenders and tipplers. The brand continues to offer consistent value across their bottlings.

ALIPÚS SANTA ANA

Hernández Melchor, Santa Ana, Oaxaca
Espadín (*A. angustifolia*)

ABV: 42%
PRICE: $$

Classic flavors of smoke and citrus. ■ Bright green vegetation and subtle smoke perfume the nose. Tropical fruit punch, red Fresno chili, and fragrant orange peel are juicy and concentrated, with whisps of violet and gardenia wafting up the throat after a sip. The suede-like finish is soft.

ALIPÚS SAN JUAN XX

Familia Antonio Juan, San Juan del Río, Oaxaca
Tepeztate, Tobala, Sierra Negra (*A. marmorata*, *A. potatorum*, *A. americana*)

ABV: 48%
PRICE: $$$$

This is the kind of wildly flavorful mezcal that draws you in ever deeper. ■ The aromas are fruity and fresh—mango cheesecake, watermelon, cucumber—with a touch of funk. Chocolatey with cinnamon, dried cherry, pineapple, and cream, the flavors are a dessert lover's dream.

ALMAMEZCALERA PAL'ALMA

Known as the Indiana Jones of mezcal, Erick Rodriguez forms deep familial connections with communities producing small-batch traditional mezcal from all over Mexico. All of the bottlings are limited quantities, and it wasn't until 2020 that they were technically available for purchase at stores and bars in the United States. Beloved in the industry, and with a reputation for sourcing the best spirits, this is a true gem of a brand that has come to be a symbol of quality and ethical practices. Across the board, these mezcals are well worth their price tags.

PAL'ALMA SALMIANA

Patricio Hernandez, San Luis Potosí
Salmiana

ABV: 50%
PRICE: $$$$

Made using 30% pulque in the fermentation, this is a last-of-its-kind bottling since Patricio passed away just before 2020. An absolute delight. ▪ Endlessly fascinating aromas of roasted green banana, cigar spice box, and peppery green herbs. The flavors burst in the mouth, cascading with dried orange and pineapple, chili-salted mango, and silken baked acorn squash. The finish is grassy and fruity with pineapple husk and a hint of pine tips.

PAL'ALMA TOBAXICHE

Apolonio y Simeón Ramírez, Ejutla, Oaxaca
Tobaxiche (*A. karwinskii*)

ABV: 56%
PRICE: $$$$

This is an ideal sipping companion to desserts and/or fine cigars. ▪ Caramelized and toasted aromas are warm and inviting with flan, caramel, and fried bananas. An impressive concentration of flavors pours over the palate, revealing chocolate, creamy coffee, fig jam, and date-filled pastries. The finish is rich with sweet roasted tobacco and lily of the valley.

PAL'ALMA PAPALOTE

Artemio García, Guerrero

Papalote (*A. cupreata*)

ABV: 50%

PRICE: $$$$

Made using three-year capon agaves and aged in glass up to twenty-eight months; the result is rich and concentrated flavors. ■ Aromatically light and fresh, with mineral and clay notes coming to the fore, and subtle herbal wafts in the background. Once in the mouth, the flavors come to life, balancing roasted chicory and other earthy roots like sweet carrots and beets, plus blood orange. The finish is crisp, light, and herby.

AMARAS

Also known as Mezcal Amores in Mexico, this brand was founded in 2010 and is run by a small group of people who have diverse backgrounds in the spirits industry. The brand offers mezcal from different states of Mexico, with a central philosophy of sustainability and giving back to the communities that produce mezcal. To this end, 15% of the profits from some of their mezcals are devoted to sustainability and community projects, such as upcycling spent agave fibers into building materials and planting agave for future harvest.

AMARAS CUPREATA VERANO

Faustino Robledo, Tixtla, Guerrero

Cupreata lot 2

ABV: 43%

PRICE: $$

A light and earthy mezcal. ■ Clean aromas of cotton and fresh linen mix with herbs and baked earth. Piquant in the mouth with a suede-like texture. The flavors of green chili, tarragon, and mint have undertones of green banana, and chayote.

BALANCAN

Founded by Ismael Gomez, Balancan is under the umbrella of Laika Spirits, which also encompasses Cruz de Fuego (page 137), and Flor del Desierto (page 213). Designed as a collection of uncertified agave spirits from different regions of Mexico, the brand is a study in the diversity that lies outside of the conventional (and legal) understanding of mezcal. The spirits are made in small and limited batches by nature, and showcase unique production techniques, traditions, and varieties.

BALANCAN TUXCA
Ignacio Juarez, Jalisco
Cimarrón and Lineño (**A. rhodacantha, A. angustifolia**)

ABV: 46%

PRICE: $$$

From the border of Jalisco and Colima, Tuxca is one of the oldest Indigenous styles of agave distillates. ■ Minerals and fresh green sweet peas are crisp and airy aromas. The texture is chalky, matching the initial spiciness on the tongue that morphs into a rounded, brown sugar-kissed earthiness. A touch of smoke lingers on the finish.

BALANCAN PAPALOME
Amando Alvarez, Santa Maria Ixcatlán, Oaxaca
Papalome (**A. cupreata**)

ABV: 46%

PRICE: $$$$

A uniquely fruity mezcal with layers of flavor in each sip. ■ Banana taffy, candied orange, and light vanilla aromas are nostalgic and intriguing. The fruit flavors are front and center, with each sip developing with baking spices, minerals, and a touch of lactic funk on the finish.

BANHEZ

Founder Francisco Javier has been involved in the mezcal industry since the 1990s, along with his brother and mother. In 2000, he helped organize a group of producers in Ejutla, Oaxaca. He noticed that working communally brought greater opportunity to each individual producer, for example, by offsetting certification and marketing costs. Banhez is a functional co-op with forty-seven producers and agave growers, mostly from Ejutla and a few from the Valles Centrales region. Mezcal Artesanal from thirty-seven palenques is blended to create a one-liter bottle, much like blended malts from Scotland. They also offer bottlings from individual producers.

BANHEZ JOVEN
Ejutla, Oaxaca
Espadín, Barril (*A. angustifolia, A. karwinskii*)

ABV: 42%
PRICE: $

A good choice for cocktails. ▪ Light and aromas are clean with a touch of lactic creaminess. Soft on the palate, flavors of charred pineapple, subtle smoke, and smooth milk chocolate.

BANHEZ TEPEZTATE
Apolonio Patricio, Ejutla, Oaxaca
Tepeztate (*A. marmorata*)

ABV: 47%
PRICE: $$$

Fiery spice dominates the flavor. ▪ Aromas of light smoke and candied watermelon rind, followed by sweet and spicy flavors—green pepper, red clay, and charred orange flesh.

BORROSO

A relatively new brand, Borroso is operated by sisters Claudia and Maria Turrent in Baja California, who contract with independent Oaxacan producers to bottle and sell artisanally made mezcal. The producers they work with generally do not have the means to create and market a brand on their own. Borroso creates a unique one-liter bottle. The spirits are made from Espadín.

BORROSO SANTIAGO MATATLÁN

Santiago Matatlán, Oaxaca

Espadín (*A. angustifolia*)

ABV: 49%	A solid mezcal that would work in a variety of refreshing cocktails or
PRICE:	enjoyed neat. ■ Rock candy and mineral aromas are light and refreshing. The flavor is zesty, with mild earthiness and green chili spice.

BOZAL

This brand is from 3 Badge Beverage Corporation, a US-based company that has a combination of wine and spirits in its portfolio. The brand focuses on wild agave varieties from across Oaxaca, Guerrero, and Durango, searching out distinctive producers to partner with for their many offerings, including regular limited releases. The bottles are striking and easy to identify; they are tall earth-toned clay vessels that are themselves works of art.

BOZAL RESERVA COYOTE

Isidro Damian, Sola de Vega, Oaxaca
Coyote (*A. americana*), lot 00420

ABV: 47%	A dynamic and vibrant sipping mezcal with an impressive range of
PRICE: $$$$	flavors and clean flavorful finish. ▪ Aromas of clay and roses, supported by refreshing fruits like cucumber, lime, and star fruit. Balanced in the mouth with flavors of passionfruit, sweet lime, almonds, and cooked agave. The finish is focused, allowing the flavors to persist on the palate with clarity.

BOZAL ENSAMBLE ESPADÍN BARRIL MEXICANO

Fermin Garcia, Adrian and Lucio Bautista, San Dionisio y Ejutla de Crespo, Oaxaca
Espadín, Barril, Mexicano (*A. angustifolia*, *A. karwinskii*, SP), lot 03921

ABV: 47%	Concentrated flavors make this a rich sipping mezcal that would
PRICE: $$	pair with decadent entrees and desserts. ▪ Mild earthy aromas with undertones of lilies and hay. Nicely concentrated flavors wash over the palate with anise, red chili spice, and white chocolate. The finish is round and ripe, with kiwi, cantaloupe, and fresh herbs.

BOZAL BORREGO SACRIFICIO

Adrian Bautista, Ejutla de Crespo, Oaxaca
Espadín, Tobala (*A. angustifolia, A. potatorum*), lot 00521

ABV: 47%	Distilled with lamb, this special edition mezcal is rich with a fatty texture
PRICE: $$	and citrus flavors. ▪ Dried citrus rind aromas jump from the glass. In the mouth, the texture is fatty and soft, allowing rich minerality, mixed citrus, and dried herb flavors to flow across the palate. The bright finish shows vanilla.

CABALLITO CERRERO

A unique spirit, Caballito Cerrero was once certified as tequila but is more accurately classified as a destilado de agave, or historical mezcal, and the company decided not to market their product as tequila from 2018 and beyond. It is produced at the Fábrica Santa Rita in Amatitán, Jalisco, which is home to a sixteenth-century archeological site for agave distillation. Alfonso Jiménez Rosales founded the brand in 1950 following a split from Herradura (page 99), a brand that he helped create. Caballito Cerrero translates to "the horse that does not need horseshoes." The spirits are made using blue weber agave as well as other typical varieties used ancestrally in the community.

CABALLITO CERRERO AZUL

Amatitán, Jalisco
Azul (**A. tequilana**)

ABV: 46%

PRICE: $$$

A delicious taste of what tequila once was. ▪ Red floral aromas mix with citrus and tropical fruit notes. The texture is silky and richly cascades over the palate. Flavors of cactus fruit, oranges, spring blossoms, and lime zest are balanced and focused.

CHACOLO

One of the tastiest spirits from Jalisco comes from a father and son team, Macario and Miguel Partida, who have been dedicated to agave stewardship and traditional production for generations. The brand and family are recognized locally and within the craft agave spirits industries as masters of their craft and pillars of their community. They use capon agaves that are left to concentrate sugars in the hearts for years, rather than the typical months, with an extra-long fermentation in volcanic rock pits. The spirits are distilled using a Filipino-style still made of copper and a hollowed-out tree trunk. With a yearly production around two thousand liters, each batch is a special release.

CHACOLO IXTERO VERDE
Macario Partida Ramos, Zapotitlán de Vadillo, Jalisco
Angustifolia

ABV: 46.5%
PRICE: $$$$

Made with a local agave variety with three years of capon. A gem. ■ Salty-sweet aromas are alluring, almost meaty and floral at once, backed by sour cream, pomelo, and dry earth. Tangy and lactic notes continue on the palate, with cheese Danish, lily of the valley, and lemon zest. The finish is mineral and chalky.

CLASE AZUL

Primarily known as a tequila brand (page 83), Clase Azul also offers limited releases of mezcal. Similarly to the tequilas, the striking clay bottle accounts for the inflated price; it comes with hand-beaded accents crafted by the Indigenous Wixárika people.

CLASE AZUL DURANGO
Durango
Cenizo (**A. durangensis**)

ABV: 40%	A soft and lightly flavored mezcal. ■ Gentle aromas of hay and fresh
PRICE: $$$$	grass. In the mouth, the flavors are muted, with chili spice and a zesty texture coming to the fore.

CONVITE

Convite is made by the Hernández family, which has deep roots in the heritage of the Oaxacan mezcal tradition, spanning five generations. In addition to artisanal mezcal production, they have nurseries that contain many different varieties of agave species and are active participants in preserving the agave biodiversity of their region. The brand offers an extensive line of varieties as well as a lower alcohol espadín-based mezcal designed for mixology.

CONVITE ESENCIAL
Cosme and Daniel Hernández San Baltazar Guelavila, Oaxaca
Espadín (**A. angustifolia**)

ABV: 38%	A nice option for cocktails. ■ Aromas are clean, showing pineapple and
PRICE: $$	hints of smoke. In the mouth the flavors are soft and delicate, with creamy minerals, roasted tropical fruits, and herbs.

CRUZ DE FUEGO

From mother and son team Margarita Blas and Carlos Mendez comes this artisanal brand of Oaxacan mezcal, made in Santiago Matatlán. Launched in 2015, Cruz de Fuego works with native varieties of agave, always produced according to the local customs, including tahona crushing and open-air wood tank fermentation with the fibers and ambient yeasts.

CRUZ DE FUEGO MADRECUISHE

Margarita Blas and Carlos Mendez, Santiago Matatlán, Oaxaca
Madrecuishe (*A. karwinskii*)

ABV: 48%

PRICE: $$$

Bursting with ripe flavors, this mezcal is easy to love. ■ Roasted earth, green plantain, and juicy pear aromas fill the glass. The flavor begins with a burst of ripe sweetness and slightly candied citrus, followed by creamy marshmallow, forest twigs, and apple skins. Gently spiced on the finish, it's a mix between baking spices and green chili.

CUERO VIEJO

This artisanal brand from Nombre de Dios, Durango was founded in 2015 by Miguel Garza after decades of dreaming it up. It's currently managed by his daughter Martha Garza. Like their friends and neighbors, the Saravia family of Origen Raíz (page 193), their vinata draws from Oaxacan techniques for production, creating a unique hybrid style. The agave used comes from community-owned and managed lands nearby, where they have long-standing relationships. They have made some experimental and traditional infusions as well as seasonal batches, which adds another layer of terroir to their releases. The vinata is part of the expansive family owned and operated ranch with a spa resort, Urajan de Luna, which features one-of-a-kind agave-themed wellness treatments that use the plant in novel ways.

CUERO VIEJO JOVEN
Francisco Camacho, Nombre de Dios, Durango
Cenizo (*A. durangensis*)

ABV: 48%
PRICE: n/a

A full-flavored mezcal from an iconic region of Durango. ■ Clay, red fruits, kiwi, and dried hay are just some of the aromas that continue to blossom from the glass. The richness takes off in the mouth, with supple yet deep notes of tobacco, dark chocolate, summer plums, dried mango, and peach. The finish shows herbs, roasted tomato, and caraway.

CUISH

Félix Hernández Monterrosa, who comes from a mezcal-producing family, founded the mezcaleria in Oaxaca in 2009. Offering much more than copitas of exclusive regional mezcals, Cuishe the bar was the first of its kind and has always been a cultural center for the art, culture, and community that accompanies traditional mezcal. Within the last few years, in partnership with Rion Toal of Maestros de Mezcal, Cuish the brand began exporting outside of Mexico. The small batches of artisanal mezcal are carefully curated to represent the unadulterated traditions of the producers.

CUISH MADRECUISHE

Hermogenes Vasquez, San Luis Amatlán, Oaxaca
Madrecuishe (**A. *karwinskii***)

ABV: 48%
PRICE: $$$$

A powerfully concentrated mezcal with mesmerizing layers of tasty fruit. ▪ Lemon and lime zest are earthy and mineral rich, rather than sweet or candied, on the nose. The flavors are deeply concentrated in the mouth, immediately filling the palate with pear, guava, raspberry, and roasted earth flavors.

CUISH ESPADÍN-MEXICANO

Francisco Garcia León, Miahuatlán, Oaxaca
Espadín, Mexicano (**A. *angustifolia*, A. *rhodacanta***)

ABV: 49%
PRICE: $$$

This mezcal transports the drinker to the palenque through flavor and aroma. ▪ The aromas are creamy with notes of crème brûlée, flan, and green asparagus. On the palate, it begins sweet and soft, with plenty of minerals and herbal notes up front. The spiciness kicks in on the finish, leaving a mild and pleasant tongue tingle.

CUISH CERRUDO 2020

Rufino Felipe Martínez, Santa Catarina Minas, Oaxaca

Cerrudo (*A. americana*)

ABV: 46%

PRICE: $$$$

An earthy mezcal through and through. ▪ Hay, dried autumn leaves, and freshly toasted tortillas are earthy aromas. A nice hit of salt opens the flavors, quickly followed by chili-spiked cucumber, clay, and chocolate. The finish is mineral-rich and long, with punctuations of cilantro and eucalyptus.

CUISH CUISH 2016

Francisco Garcia León, Miahuatlán, Oaxaca

Cuish (*A. karwinskii*)

ABV: 46%

PRICE: $$$

A savory and rustic mezcal. ▪ Leather, musk, and sweet pipe tobacco remain mild aromatically, though beautifully integrated. In the mouth, the flavors of lime sorbet, green bell pepper, dill, and celery skew savory. The texture is rustic, reminiscent of a cobblestone path.

CUISH ESPADÍN CAPON 2004

José Santiago López, Santiago Matatlán, Oaxaca

Espadín (*A. angustifolia*)

ABV: 45%

PRICE: $$$$

An example of how mind-bendingly delicious non-wood aged mezcal can be; this is aged fifteen years in stainless steel. ▪ Blackberry jam and candy, roses, and candied hibiscus are deeply concentrated aromas. It is light and lively on the palate; a touch of red chili spice dances around as flavors of chocolate-covered raspberries and sugar plums fill the mouth. Woodsy rosemary and other herbs add depth to the finish.

DEL MAGUEY

Del Maguey is perhaps the most recognized brand of mezcal throughout the world, easily spotted in its distinctive green bottle. The brand was born from the spirited travels of artist Ron Cooper, who made deep connections with Zapotec communities of Oaxaca that blossomed into a business in the mid-1990s. Credited with introducing the US bar scene to true artisanal mezcal, unadulterated and unchanged for the foreign palate, Ron and the small Del Maguey team went door-to-door with mezcal from small villages of Oaxaca. While only a few industry professionals understood how special and unique the spirits were, it was enough to keep the brand alive, and in many ways it sparked the exponential growth of interest in traditional mezcal we see today. While the brand has grown from a grassroots effort to an international business, many offerings from the brand continue to reflect the heritage of mezcal from the communities that have been making it for centuries.

DEL MAGUEY VIDA DE MUERTOS

Paciano Cruz Nolasco, San Luis del Río, Oaxaca
Espadín (*A. angustifolia*), lot 211

ABV: 45%	A higher alcohol, seasonal autumn distilled sibling of the classic Vida
PRICE: $$	bottling. ■ Mixed citrus, soursop, and a touch of heady ferment funk aromas are enthralling. Refreshing cucumber, lime zest, smoked sea salt, and dragon fruit are gently sweet and soft on the palate. The finish is flavorful, with almond and roasted orange zest.

DEL MAGUEY CHICHICAPA

Faustino Garcia Vasquez, San Baltazar Chichicapam, Oaxaca
Espadín (*A. angustifolia*)

ABV: 48%	A classic with cult favorite status, the signature dark-roasted agaves
PRICE: $$$	create a caramelized flavor profile. ■ Toasted nuts, caramelized pineapple, and charred pine needles are rich aromas. Earthy, nutty, and sweet flavors meld together, delivering baking spices, chocolate, tobacco, and coffee, while retaining an earthy core of minerals and herbs. Smooth, lightly spiced, and long on the finish.

DEL MAGUEY SANTO DOMINGO ALBARRADAS

Espiridion Morales Luis, Santo Domingo Albarradas, Oaxaca
Espadín (**A. angustifolia**), lot 154

ABV: 48%

PRICE: $$$

Focused aromas and flavors show off the diversity of what can hide within a single spirit. ▪ Heady aromas of tropical fruits and flowers are delicious. The flavor is equally beguiling, showing green cactus fruit, starfruit, grapefruit zest, minerals, and a touch of brown sugar. The texture is soft, with a gentle spice that plays on the tongue. Citrus and honeysuckle linger on the crisp finish.

DEL MAGUEY TOBALA

Rogelio Martinez Cruz, Santa María Albarradas, Oaxaca
Tobala (**A. potatorum**), lot 181

ABV: 45%

PRICE: $$$$

The layers of smoke and fresh agave create a beguiling harmony of flavors. ▪ The aromas are ethereal, leading with minerality and sweet fruits like kiwi and finger limes. Supremely silken on the tongue, the fresh minerals, sea salt, and tomatillo flavors turn to campfire, berries, and mango. The smooth finish is almost peaty, with rich leather.

DEL MAGUEY ARROQUEÑO

Luis Carlos Vasquez, Santa Catarina Minas, Oaxaca
Arroqueño (**A. americana**), lot 126

ABV: 49%

PRICE: $$$$

An iconic and memorable mezcal that captures the delicious traditions of Minas in every sip. ▪ Sweet aromas of macerated strawberries, pound cake, and jackfruit are buttery and indulgent. The clay and mineral notes hit the palate first, expanding outward with gentle spice, creamy almond, pineapple chutney, and plantain. The finish is caramelized with almonds and chocolate.

DEL MAGUEY WILD TEPEXTATE

Rogelio Martinez Cruz, Santa María Albarradas, Oaxaca

Tepextate (**A. marmorata**), lot 171

ABV: 45%

PRICE: $$$$

A fruity and earthy layered mezcal whose characteristics are brought to life when paired with chocolate. ■ Hickory nuts, smoked pecan, and pickled watermelon rind are bright, and roasted earthy aromas. The soft chalky texture pleasantly coats the palate, filling the mouth with flavors of charred earth, watermelon, berries, and hibiscus. The warm finish is kissed with citrus.

DEL MAGUEY MINERO

Luis Carlos Vasquez, Santa Catarina Minas, Oaxaca

Espadín (**A. angustifolia**), lot 192

ABV: 50%

PRICE: $$$

Distilled in clay pots, this mezcal would pair well with anything grilled or coffee-flavored. ■ Mixed peppercorns, olive brine, and deli meat are savory aromas that hide just beneath the strong alcohol. Tart and spicy, the leathery texture delivers flavors of orange zest, coffee, and pomegranate arils. The finish is herbal, with rosemary, chervil, and cooling lemon balm.

DEL MAGUEY WILD PAPALOME

Fernando Caballero Cruz, San Pedro Teozacoalco, Oaxaca

Papalome (**A. cupreata**), lot 161

ABV: 45%

PRICE: $$$$

Deeply roasted and caramelized flavors are balanced with fruit and custard notes; pair this one with dessert. ■ Tropical and orchard fruit aromas enjoy a layer of depth from a touch of funkiness. The velvety texture is full of crunchy oats, smoked quinoa, and roasted pears. Creamy flan with a burnt caramel top makes for a scrumptious finish.

DEL MAGUEY PECHUGA

Florencio Carlos Sarmiento (Don Lencho), Santa Catarina Minas, Oaxaca

Espadín (*A. angustifolia*), lot 131

ABV: 49%
PRICE: $$$$

Distilled in clay pots with apple, plums, pineapple, plantains, almonds, and a chicken breast in the third distillation. ■ Mostly fruit aromas mix with clay minerality. Pillowy soft on the palate, with round juicy flavors of orchard fruits, almonds, vanilla, anise, and sweet oak abounding. There is an oiliness that coats the palate, leaving an herbaceous and star anise character to the silken finish.

DEL MAGUEY IBÉRICO

Luis Carlos Vasquez, Santa Catarina Minas, Oaxaca

Espadín (*A. angustifolia*), lot 191

ABV: 49%
PRICE: $$$$

Clay pot distilled with seasonal fruits and jamón ibérico in the third distillation. ■ Spicy aromas of artichoke, anise, and clove are seductively unique. The flavors of baking spices, bergamot, pine, and fine cured ham permeate each sip, along with a subtle layer of fattiness that adds to the indulgently rich profile. A one-of-a-kind mezcal worth trying.

DEL MAGUEY SAN PABLO AMEYALTEPEC

Aurelio Gonzalez Tobon, San Pablo Ameyaltepec, Puebla

Papalote (*A. potatorum*), lot 171

ABV: 47%
PRICE: $$$$

A delicious mezcal from Puebla. ■ Blackberries, dark honey, and freshly cut grass are equally sweet and earthy aromas. Salted caramel, peach candy, pineapple, and coconut cream flavors cascade over the palate in a whirlwind of juicy flavors that continue to unfold. Endlessly sippable.

DERRUMBES

Derrumbes was one of the first brands to offer a sampling of mezcal from the states that are rarely seen on the shelves, such as San Luis Potosí, Zacatecas, and Tamaulipas. The project was founded by Esteban Morales, owner of La Venenosa Raicilla (page 216), and Sergio Mendoza, owner of Don Fulano Tequila (page 88). They partner with producers from across different states, creating a lineup of artisanal mezcals that show off the techniques and varieties distinct to each region. Their mezcals offer a lot of value.

DERRUMBES MICHOACÁN
Lupe Pérez Toledo, Tzitzio, Michoacán
Cupreata, Inaequidens

ABV: 45%
PRICE: $$$

Produced using a wooden hat still and rested in glass before release. ■ Citrus and flowers characterize the nose. In the mouth, the flavors skew herbal, with cucumber, lemon, tarragon, and sweet basil. Hints of spice and acidity keep the flavors ever fresh in the mouth, with a crisp finish of stone fruits and smoke.

DERRUMBES DURANGO
Uriel Simental, Nombre de Dios, Durango
Cenizo Durangensis

ABV: 45%
PRICE: $$$

A dynamic mezcal with sweet and savory flavors. ■ Caramelized with a touch of saltiness, the aromas are layered, much like the flavors to come. Concentrated umami notes suggest cured meats, mixing with black pepper, citrus, and peach flavors. The finish is full of minerals and clay.

DERRUMBES ZACATECAS
Jaime Bañuelos, Juitzila, Zacatecas
Tequilana Weber Azul

ABV: 42%
PRICE: $$$

Hails from a region that is similar to tequila but produced in an ancient fashion. ■ Lime zest and mild campfire aromas are bright and inviting. Sturdy flavors are earthy, with charred leaves, lime leaf, baked citrus, pink peppercorn, and smoked paprika. The finish is peppery with candied orange.

DERRUMBES OAXACA

Javier Mateo, Santiago Matatlán, Oaxaca

Espadín, Tobala (**A. angustifolia, A. potatorum**)

ABV: 48%	
PRICE: $$$	

Fermented with the addition of pulque, this is a complex and layered mezcal. ■ Earth and smoke are front and center aromatically, with fruity and floral undertones. The flavors are smooth and chocolatey, with coffee, black pepper, roasted red fruits, and roasted pineapple. A classic and easy-drinking mezcal.

DERRUMBES SAN LUIS POTOSÍ

Juan Manuel Pérez, Charcas, San Luis Potosí

Salmiana Crassispina

ABV: 43%	
PRICE: $$	

Produced using agaves cooked in an aboveground oven, it has a less smoky flavor profile. ■ Green and vegetal aromas have overtones of minerals and tangy fruits. It is a touch spicy in the mouth, and the flavors soften into anise, chalky minerals, coffee, and brown sugar-candied orange peel. The finish is long and flavorful.

DERRUMBES TAMAULIPAS

Cuauhtémoc Jacques, San Carlos, Tamaulipas

Amole, Amole, Americana (**A. funkiana, A. univittata, A. americana**)

ABV: 46.1%	
PRICE: $$$	

Featuring high-toned aromas and fermented flavors; this is a spirit for the adventurous. ■ Aromas are ripe with tropical fruits, fermented plant material, and a healthy dose of funk. Similar on the palate, with more tropical fruits, exotic blossoms, kiwi, green coffee bean, and aromatic grapes. Minerals and chocolate are rich on the finish.

DIVINO MAGUEY

Divino Maguey is owned by two friends from Yucatán who have been involved in the Oaxacan mezcal industry since 2010. After starting a small bottling company in 2015, they purchased Divino Maguey in 2016 and now export the brand to Europe, Africa, and the Americas.

DIVINO MAGUEY CUISHE

San Dionisio Ocotepec, Oaxaca

Cuishe (*A. karwinskii*)

ABV: 47%

PRICE: $$$

Show off the flavors by pairing with equally boldly flavored dishes. ▪ The heady aroma of fresh green peas and sweet dried flowers is intoxicating. Tastes like dried fruit velvet, juicy blood orange, and blackberry. The hickory-kissed finish is softly smoked with notes of green tree branches.

DIXEEBE

The name of this brand is a Zapotec word that means much more than "cheers." It's an expression of gratitude toward all of the people and circumstances that make a celebratory moment possible. Asis Cortés has become known for spreading this good cheer internationally, often with mezcal from his father, Valentin Cortés, in hand. Along with Origen Raíz (page 193), Dixeebe is the central focus for the highly renowned father and son team whose roots with mezcal can be traced back to at least 1840. Upon launching, there were nine small-batch expressions available for preorder. As a highly sought after brand, these are difficult to find, and worth grabbing a bottle or two when you do.

DIXEEBE TOBALA
Valentin Cortés, Santiago Matatlán, Oaxaca
Tobala (**A. potatorum**)

ABV: 49%
PRICE: $$$

An intriguing mezcal that opens up in many layers; the more you sip, the more you discover. ▪ Spicy and green aromas of Thai basil and lime leaf are uplifting and fresh. The texture starts out pillowy and then turns slightly leathery, delivering flavors of green melon, apples, plantain, and lilies. The earthy sweet flavors are balanced and integrated and leave the mouth feeling clean.

DIXEEBE PULQUERO
Valentin Cortés, Santiago Matatlán, Oaxaca
Pulquero (**A. americana**)

ABV: 51%
PRICE: $$$

Made from agave typically used for pulque, this is a crisp and refreshing mezcal. ▪ Aromas of cotton are light and airy. Sweet cactus fruit, cucumber, and dried orange are earthy and sweet flavors, lightly coating the palate. Dusty spice lingers on the tongue, as perfumed floral aromas mix with kiwi, dragon fruit, and pomelo.

DIXEEBE MADRECUISHE

Valentin Cortés, Santiago Matatlán, Oaxaca

Madrecuishe (*A. karwinskii*)

ABV: 49%

PRICE: $$$

Robust and bright, this is a tart and fruity sipper. ■ Wet earth aromas are lightly smoked, with green tobacco leaf and green banana peel. Tart and bright, the flavors are full of juicy citrus, nectarine skin, overripe pineapple, and dried papaya. The fruity notes turn to satiny spice on the finish.

DIXEEBE TEPEZTATE

Valentin Cortés, Santiago Matatlán, Oaxaca

Tepeztate (*A. marmorata*)

ABV: 47.6%

PRICE: $$$

A classic tepeztate with undertones of brie cheese and white pepper. ■ Full and fragrant with blackberries and blueberries, juicy melons, slate, and graphite. A never-ending list of flavors unfolds with each sip, revealing pears, pineapple, salted Brazil nuts, chayote, creamy bloomy rind cheese, cracked wheat, and white pepper. The finish is spiced and mineral.

DON AMADO

Don Amado is made in Santa Catarina Minas by the Arellanas family using traditional clay pot distillation. The family has been making regional mezcal for eleven generations, with recognition from the community that goes back to the 1700s. As a longtime friend of the family, Jake Lustig of Haas Brothers (pages 97) not only imports the brand but also was instrumental in bringing it to fruition. While not technically producer owned, the profit-sharing model ensures that the Arellanas family directly and freely enjoys the financial profits from the brand. The mezcals carry that special flavor from the ancestral clay pot distillation technique.

DON AMADO TOBALA AND BICUISHE ENSEMBLE

Germaín Arellanes Arellanes, Santa Catarina Minas, Oaxaca
Tobala, Bicuishe (*A. potatorum, A. karwinskii*)

ABV: 46%

PRICE: $$$

Made in Minas with agave sourced from San Pablo Apostol, it is full of classic Minas flavor. ■ Aromas are on the subtle side with dried fruits, sea salt, and fresh sourdough bread. The flavor comes on slowly, gentle at first, and then swelling to a crescendo of green fruits, mineral water, and dried pineapple. A gentle smokiness permeates the finish alongside strawberry and pink peppercorn.

DON AMADO ARROQUEÑO

Germaín Arellanes Arellanes, Santa Catarina Minas, Oaxaca
Arroqueño (*A. americana*)

ABV: 46%

PRICE: $$$

Ripe and fruity, this expressive mezcal has focused and clean flavors. ■ Boiled potatoes, clay, and other earthy aromas swirl in the glass. Ripe flavors of custard apple, berries, and star fruit are creamy and citric, giving way to sweet green leaves, pear skin, and blanched almonds. The finish is kissed with cherry and almond.

DON AMADO PECHUGA

Germaín Arellanes Arellanes, Santa Catarina Minas, Oaxaca

Espadín (*A. angustifolia*)

ABV: 45%

PRICE: $$$$

This is a third distillation of their Rustico mezcal, with the addition of autumnal wild fruits, nuts, and spices. Always excellent. ■ Dried fruit aromas have herbal undertones. Balanced and integrated flavors of pineapple, raisin, raspberry, almond, clay, apple, and anise are smooth and creamy. The full body is a touch oily, creating a luxurious mouthfeel. The finish continues to offer layers of fresh and dried fruit flavors.

DON MATEO

From the Vieyra family in Michoacán, Don Mateo represents six generations as stewards of the land and makers of mezcal—at times in secret under threat of persecution. Their ranch where the agaves come from doubles as a nature preserve, often visited by local scientists and academics for research. At the helm is maestro mezcalero Emilio Vieyra, carrying on the legacy of his late father, José Emilio Vieyra Rangel. His mother, Delia Vargas Vieyra, herself the granddaughter of a mezcalero, is the president of the Women's Association of Mezcal Producers in Michoacán and is an undeniable matriarch and mentor in the world of mezcal. The mezcals are benchmark examples of what Michoacán has to offer, both in flavors and heritage.

DON MATEO CUPREATA
Emilio Vieyra, Pino Bonito, Michoacán
Cupreata, lot 25

ABV: 46%
PRICE: $$$

An instant classic, this spirit is a wonderful introduction to the mezcals of Michoacán. ■ Aromas of freshly fallen rain, minerals, sweet water, and dried grass are subtle and elegant. The mouth bursts with lively flavors of baked squash, melon, green chilies, and fire-roasted yellow tomato. The finish is silken and grapey.

DON MATEO PECHUGA
Emilio Vieyra, Pino Bonito, Michoacán
Cupreata, lot D-42

ABV: 45%
PRICE: $$$$

A benchmark pechuga, the recipe of matriarch Delia Vargas Vieyra, grab this for special celebrations. ■ Aromas of fresh spring water, minerals, baking spices, and green fruits. Slightly sweet on the palate with notes of pineapple and mango amid roasted red chilies, cinnamon, mace, and wet clay. The sweet spices linger on the finish, whirling up even more layers of flavor.

DOS PASIONES

Epigmenio Martinez Pérez, now in his nineties, has been a lifelong mezcalero, and he continues to be involved in production alongside his sons Edgar and Diego. After decades of selling his mezcal to other brands, he and his sons decided to create their own brand to showcase his experience and mastery of distilling agave. The name, meaning "two passions," represents that he has another lifelong passion: he is just as renowned for his musical talents and teaching abilities as he is for his mezcal. Dos Pasiones is part of the new wave of small producer-owned brands that are proud to share their culture directly, rather than selling to companies that often mix their small lots into larger batches.

DOS PASIONES TEPEZTATE
Epigmenio Martinez Pérez, Santa María Albarradas, Oaxaca
Tepeztate (*A. marmorata*)

ABV: Unknown	A mineral and fruit driven mezcal. ▪ Fruity aromas are full of berries
PRICE: n/a	and classic watermelon rind notes. In the mouth, the flavors are kissed with vanilla, minerals, and sweet herbs. The finish is lightly spicy with zesty orange.

EL BUHO

El Buho is made in Matatlán, Oaxaca, by the Jimenez Mendez family, fifth-generation distillers committed to traditional production methods. Founded in 2010 by US-based acclaimed chef TJ Steele, the brand offers a lineup of artisanally produced mezcals that feature the agave biodiversity of the region. The offerings include a cocktail-driven mezcal as well as special releases.

EL BUHO ESPADÍN CAPÓN

Octavio Jimenez Monterroza, Santiago Matatlán, Oaxaca

Espadín (**A. angustifolia**)

ABV: 47%

PRICE: $$$

Made from one-year capon agaves, this expression is deep in flavor. ▪ Bold, smoky aromas of roasted pineapple, red fruits, and sunbaked earth. Minerals are front and center on the palate, matching the creamy texture with layers of tropical fruits, vanilla custard, and green grapes. The soft clay finish is endless.

EL BUHO ENSEMBLE

Octavio Jimenez Monterroza, Santiago Matatlán, Oaxaca

Americana (**A. karwinskii**)

ABV: 50%

PRICE: $$$

A scrumptious blend that serves as dessert on its own. ▪ Lightly caramelized aromas offer banana bread and flan, with earthy tobacco undertones. The play between sweet and charred flavors is balanced in the mouth, with a velvety texture that enhances the dessert-like flavors.

EL BUHO ARROQUEÑO

Octavio Jimenez Monterroza, Santiago Matatlán, Oaxaca

Arroqueño (**A. americana**)

ABV: 53%

PRICE: $$$$

Made in Matatlán from agaves sourced from San Baltazar Guelavila. ▪ Spicy aromas have meaty and fruity undertones, promising a diverse range of flavors. It does not disappoint in the mouth, overflowing with rounded notes of blueberry, savory cured meats, and woodsy herbs.

EL BUHO TEPEZTATE

Octavio Jimenez Monterroza, Santiago Matatlán, Oaxaca

Tepeztate (**A. marmorata**)

ABV: 48%

PRICE: $$$$

This triple-distilled mezcal was made in Matatlán from agave sourced from Santa María Zoquitlán. ▪ Classic fruity aromas have distinct earthy and mineral overtones. The flavors are crisp and bright, and electrifying acidity leads to a cascade of mouthwatering berries, melons, clay, and hibiscus. The finish is caramelized with piloncillo and red chili spice.

EL JOLGORIO

El Jolgorio was created by the Cortés family, who have been influential members of the Oaxacan mezcal community for generations. This wild agave–focused, ultra-premium brand falls under the Casa Cortés umbrella company, which also includes Agave de Cortes and Nuestra Soledad (page 192). It helped set the international market's standard for premium mezcal. At its inception, the brand was built around the mezcals from Valentin Cortés, Asis's father and one of the most celebrated contemporary producers, along with a few close friends and family producers from different regions of Oaxaca. While Valentin and Asis now focus on Origen Raíz (page 193) and Dixeebe (page 148), Valentin's brother Rolando continues to manage the satellite producers as well as the family palenque in Matatlán. The brand is easily recognized by the hand-designed eye-catching labels.

EL JOLGORIO TEPEXTATE 22
Rafael Mendez Cruz, San Luis del Río, Oaxaca
Tepextate (*A. marmorata*)

ABV: 48%
PRICE: $$$$

An indulgent and uniquely flavored mezcal. ▪ Bubblegum, daffodils, crushed pearl minerality, aloe. Vibrant, alive, and vinous. Spicy and inky, blackberry, fruit leather, coffee, roasted dandelion.

EL JOLGORIO TOBASICHE 9
Tio Pedro Vásquez, Miahuatlán, Oaxaca
Tobasiche (*A. karwinskii*)

ABV: 52%
PRICE: $$$$

Always a limited bottling, this is best enjoyed with dear friends and on special occasions. ▪ Clay, green plantain, sweet orange, and cilantro all play together on the nose. In the mouth, it is cooling, mineral, and fresh. The slow spice is matched with dried berry acidity, all amid a cloud-like texture.

EL MERO MERO MEZCAL

In operation since 2011, this artisanal mezcal brand is a relative newcomer to the US market.

EL MERO MERO TEPEXTATE

Justino Garcia Cruz, San Dionisio Ocotepec, Oaxaca

Tepextate (*A. marmorata*), lot 18

ABV: 48%

PRICE: $$$$

A sturdy and penetrating mezcal, pair it with chocolate-espresso torte to take it to the next level. ▪ Ripe mango and tropical fruit custard are creamy and vaguely sweet aromas. Smooth and rich, the flavors are ripe with dark green leafy vegetables, coffee, brown sugar, dried mango, and lime leaf.

EL MERO MERO TOBALA

Justino Garcia Cruz, San Dionisio Ocotepec, Oaxaca

Tobala (*A. potatorum*)

ABV: 48%

PRICE: $$$

Bold and exciting, this mezcal does not disappoint. ▪ Aloe and green peppercorns are gentle aromas. Piquant and smooth along the edges, notes of saltwater taffy, chicory, and sage combine elegantly. The bold flavors develop on the palate, deepening with cacao nib and fire-roasted red pepper.

EL REY ZAPOTECO

This family and producer-owned brand from Santiago Matatlán launched in 1960. Produced by the Hernandez Escobar family, led by matriarch Juanita, the family and brand have been around to see many iterations of the mezcal industry. Their continued presence and success in the international market is a testament to the quality in the bottle. They use estate-grown agaves as well as wild-harvested agaves in their lineup of artisanal Oaxacan mezcals.

EL REY ZAPOTECO TEPEZTATE

Hernandez Escobar Family, Santiago Matatlán, Oaxaca
Tepeztate (**A. m**_armorata_), lot 2019 E-124

ABV: 48%

PRICE: $$$

A spicy and bright tepeztate. ▪ The aromas are not particularly fruity, rather spicy and mineral-driven with salty undertones. Still spicy in the mouth, the texture is creamy, creating a nice push and pull. Blood orange, smoked meat, and raspberry are punchy and bright flavors.

EL REY ZAPOTECO ESPADÍN

Hernandez Escobar Family, Santiago Matatlán, Oaxaca
Espadín (**A. angustifolia**), lot 2021 E-130

ABV: 45%

PRICE: $$

A classic Oaxacan espadín. This would be an ideal introduction to mezcal or an all-purpose bottle. ▪ Light aromas are reminiscent of ripe pineapple and gently floral. Crushed rock, pineapple husk, and orange zest are balanced flavors, with overtones of vanilla and orange peel.

EL REY ZAPOTECO PECHUGA

Hernandez Escobar Family, Santiago Matatlán, Oaxaca
Espadín (**A. angustifolia**), lot E-128

ABV: **45%**

PRICE: $$$

The silky texture and soft spices make this an easy sipper. ▪ Sweet spices and orchard fruits come through on the nose. A silky texture is interwoven with flavors of dried citrus, pear, and smoked meats. The finish is soft with cardamom and cotton.

FAROLITO

Farolito is the hotly anticipated exported brand from Ulises Torrentera and Sandra Ortiz Brena's In Situ mezcaleria in Oaxaca. Well known in the world of mezcal, Ulises and Sandra are like godparents to many mezcal-obsessed locals and visitors. Known for the massive collection of rare and varied distillates, In Situ is a community hub for mezcaleros and the agave curious, and where many of us have bought some of the best bottles we've ever tasted. Farolito is a small way to extend their offerings to the bars and shelves outside of Oaxaca. All offerings are extremely limited releases and can be difficult to find, but they are well worth the splurge if you do.

FAROLITO PENCA VERDE
Valentin Celis, Zimatlán, Oaxaca
Penca Verde (sp. unclassified)

ABV: 45.5%
PRICE: $$$$

A sophisticated tiny batch mezcal meant for sipping. ■ Aromas of saddle leather, honeysuckle, and roasted pineapple. Full bodied with flavors of sandalwood, tobacco, and wet soil; rock sugar and red chili heat are sweet and warming on the finish.

FIDENCIO

Enrique Jimenez is the maestro mezcalero and owning partner of Fidencio, based in Santiago Matatlán, Oaxaca. Enrique is the son of Isaac Jimenez Mendez, a well-known mezcalero and co-founder of El Buho Mezcal (page 153), representing a strong family heritage. The brand is named for Enrique's great-great-grandfather Fidencio and launched in 2009 with co-owner Arik Torren, who imports agave spirits from all over Mexico, including Derrumbes (page 145), Rancho Tepua Bacanora (page 218), Sotol La Higuera (page 214), and La Venenosa Raicilla (page 216). Arik is a pioneer of importing and educating on agave spirits that fall outside the category of Mezcal. Fidencio uses estate-grown espadín and features all-capon agaves.

FIDENCIO ESPADÍN ÚNICO

Enrique Jimenez, Santiago Matatlán, Oaxaca

Espadín (*A. angustifolia*)

ABV: 40%

PRICE: $$

A refreshing, spicy mezcal. ■ Light aromas of roasted pineapple are bright and fresh. Smooth and chalky in the mouth. Flavors of melon, citrus, and minerals get a spicy kick on the back end. The finish is minerally and lightly sweet with cactus fruit and cucumber.

FIDENCIO TOBALA

Enrique Jimenez, Santiago Matatlán, Oaxaca

Tobala (*A. potatorum*)

ABV: 45%

PRICE: $$$$

A mezcal that incorporates many different flavors amid a soft texture. ■ Toasted brioche, vanilla custard, and streusel topping are inviting aromas. A pillowy texture fills the mouth with flavors of pear and pastry. Distinctly less sweet and more earthy in flavor than in aroma. Strong minerality on the finish shows notes of autumn leaves and smoked sea salt.

FIDENCIO TEPEXTATE

Enrique Jimenez, Santiago Matatlán, Oaxaca

Tepextate (*A. marmorata*)

ABV: 48%

PRICE: $$$$

Layers of flavor are generous. ■ Baked earth, dried citrus, a touch of funk, and cherries are unique aromas, reminiscent of Chianti. The flavor stretches over the palate, with warm baking spices, cranberry, and earthy steamed artichoke.

FIDENCIO MADRECUIXE

Enrique Jimenez, Santiago Matatlán, Oaxaca

Madrecuixe (*A. karwinskii*)

ABV: 45%

PRICE: $$$$

Bold flavors that reveal themselves endlessly. ■ Rich with umami aromas of smoked meats and dried red flowers. Deeply concentrated flavors of plums, herbs, clay, and mint all work together, revealing themselves in layers. The finish is long and flavorful, with a pine and minty overtone.

FIDENCIO PECHUGA

Enrique Jimenez, Santiago Matatlán, Oaxaca

Espadín (*A. angustifolia*)

ABV: 45%

PRICE: $$$

A sweet and savory pechuga. ■ Fruit notes mix with olive brine, adding interest and depth to the aromas. In the mouth, the flavors are rich with cinnamon, orange blossom, thyme, and milk chocolate. The finish is creamy and kissed with spice.

GEÜ BEEZ

Owned and operated by the García Méndez family in San Dionisio Ocotepec, Oaxaca, Geü Beez translates to "river of wasps." With generations of tradition, this Zapotec family endeavor gained certification and readied for export in 2018; the brand creates traditional sipping mezcals in small batches, prioritizing quality over quantity.

GEÜ BEEZ ESPADÍN

Crispín García Méndez, San Dionisio Ocotepec, Oaxaca

Espadín (*A. angustifolia*), lot 02

ABV: 50%

PRICE: $$

A lively and spicy mezcal that tastes like pure cooked agave. ■ Cooked agave aromas are sweet and earthy. The flavors are bold and have an earthy rusticity that is reminiscent of a traditional palenque. Notes of green mango, serrano, plantains, and tarragon are kissed with sea salt. Piquant finish.

GUSTO HISTÓRICO

This is the newest project from Marco Ochoa, co-founder of well-known Oaxacan mezcaleria Mezcaloteca and corresponding exported brand Mescalosfera. Drawing on his deep connections with producers from all over Mexico, this uncertified brand seeks out small-batch lots of mezcal that capture the brand's namesake: historical taste. Embodying the deep yet fleeting beauty of one-off batches, each bottling is a completely unique product and, more often than not, impossibly delicious.

GUSTO HISTÓRICO JUAN VÁZQUEZ

Juan Vázquez, Miahuatlán, Oaxaca

Tepextate, Tobala, Cuixe, Madrecuixe (*A. marmorata, A. potatorum, A. karwinskii, A. karwinskii*)

ABV: 48.8%
PRICE: $$$$

A tiny-batch release, full of never-ending layers of flavor and nuance. ▪ Ripe tropical fruits with mango, custard apples, and pawpaw are creamy and sweet aromas, with a touch of fermented funk. The texture is satiny smooth on the tongue, unveiling flavors of pine, pineapple husk, chocolate, roasted plums, and eucalyptus. The finish is herbal and zesty.

ILEGAL

Ilegal was founded by John Rexer in 2006 after a two-year stint bringing mezcal from Oaxaca down to his Guatemalan bar, Café No Sé. Since its inception, the brand has taken a stance on social justice issues, including pro–immigrant rights marketing campaigns, funding for Planned Parenthood, and environmental cleanup initiatives. One of the most widely available and well-known brands of mezcal, it is still produced at Mal de Amor, a Zapotec family owned and family operated palenque in Santiago Matatlán, Oaxaca, and widely used as a cocktail mezcal.

ILEGAL JOVEN
Alvaro and Armando Hernandez, Santiago Matatlán, Oaxaca
Espadín (*A. angustifolia*)

ABV: 40%

PRICE: $$

This is made in a smooth style to appeal to a wide audience. ■ Earthy aromas of pineapple husk, dry soil, and autumn leaves. Tangy in the mouth, flavors of orange and lemon give way to fiery serrano, milk chocolate, and creamy coffee. The finish is soft, returning full circle to dry earth.

LÁGRIMAS DE DOLORES

With the most comprehensive offering of mezcal from Durango to date, Lágrimas de Dolores was also one of the first mezcals from this state of northern Mexico to be exported to the United States. Started as a passion project by the Gutiérrez family in 2010 at their family owned seventeenth-century Hacienda de Dolores just outside of the city center, the brand is operated by German Gutiérrez. The majority of their spirits, including their flagship mezcals, are made at a custom-built distillery at the hacienda under the management of first-generation master distiller Fabiola Ávila. In recent years, they have expanded to include limited releases from neighboring regions, including Mezquital and Nombre de Dios, featuring other master distillers and agave terroir. Lágrimas de Dolores has bottled and released over thirteen varieties of mezcal, including some that use previously uncategorized varieties of agave. They are a founding member of Mezcales de Durango, an organization that works cooperatively and is involved in education, promotion, and growth of the category.

LÁGRIMAS DE DOLORES CENIZO

Fabiola Ávila, Durango, Durango
Cenizo Durangensis

ABV: 47%
PRICE: $$

A benchmark example of the main variety from Durango, and my personal house mezcal. ■ Aromatically mild, gentle aromas of wildflowers and fresh spring breeze are airy and refreshing. The silky texture matches the rich body. Floating flavors of wet earth, freshly split wood, coffee, and sea salted caramel. The chocolatey and hay finish shows off the earthy sweetness.

CENIZO COLONIAL TEMOAYA

Enrique de la Cruz, Temoaya, Durango
Cenizo Durangensis

ABV: 43%
PRICE: $$

One of the best values to be found for an all-purpose mezcal; good for sipping and mixing. ■ Earthy clay, wet grass, and slatey minerals are sturdy and clean aromas. Vibrant and tangy. Flavors of pineapple and tart green apple mix with coffee and dark chocolate. A hint of tobacco is ever so slightly smoky.

LÁGRIMAS DE DOLORES CASTILLA

Fabiola Ávila, Durango, Durango

Castilla (**A. angustifolia**)

ABV: 47%

PRICE: $$$

An easy-drinking mezcal made from a variety in the same family as espadín. ■ Robust aromas of dried cherries, hickory smoke, and blackberry jam. Cinnamon blankets the tongue, followed by blood orange, tart berries, and cantaloupe. A hint of vanilla and pastry cream create a sweet finish.

LÁGRIMAS DE DOLORES MASPARILLO

Familias de la Cruz and Flores, Temoaya, Durango

Masparillo (**A. maximiliana**)

ABV: 47%

PRICE: $$$

A terroir-specific variety, this demonstrates how mezcal is so much more than smoke driven flavors. ■ Complex aromas of roasted coffee and cacao nib combine with earthy green tomato and sweet caramel. Spicy and sweet with a silky texture on the palate. Sweet almond and young ginger add some freshness to the overall rich flavors.

LÁGRIMAS DE DOLORES I'GOK

Fabiola Ávila, Durango, Durango

I'gok (**A. americana**)

ABV: 47%

PRICE: $$$$

A complex sipping spirit made from a variety typically harvested for fibers. A unique treat. ■ Aromas of buttered toast, dried mango, and daffodils are enticing. The palate shows flavors of tropical fruits, brioche, citrus, and chili pepper. The endless finish is full of flowers and herbs.

LÁGRIMAS DE DOLORES VERDE

Gilberto Roldán, Nombre de Dios, Durango

Verde (**A. salmiana crassispina**)

ABV: 47%

PRICE: $$$

Of all the mezcals, this is my favorite. Made from a variety of wild agave that is rarely made into mezcal, and even more rarely exported. ■ Ethereal aromas of herbs, melon, and a hint of eucalyptus are captivating. Sea salt hits the palate and then converts to a velvety texture with flavors of berries, citrus, clay, and flowers. The juicy fruit linger after each sip, filling the mouth with watermelon, strawberry, toffee, and plantain.

LÁGRIMAS DE DOLORES TEPEMETE

Familias de la Cruz and Flores, Temoaya, Durango

Tepemete (**A. angustifolia**)

ABV: 47%

PRICE: $$$$

Pair this with young cheeses or fresh seafood to draw out the delicate notes. ■ Fresh aromas of minerals, flower stems, cucumber skin, and green mango are light yet pungent, with a hint of earthiness underneath. Clean minerals characterize the flavor as well. Spicy citrus expands over the tongue as the flavors of green herbs develop before returning to earthy slate notes.

LÁGRIMAS DE DOLORES AÑEJO

Fabiola Ávila, Durango, Durango

Cenizo Durangensis

ABV: 47%

PRICE: $$$

If ever there was a wood aged mezcal to try, this is it. ■ Woodsy aromas include vanilla, citrus, fresh pine, cereal grains, and saddle leather. The spiciness of agave remains intact while supporting notes of cedar, caramel, and coffee. Cigar box notes balance nicely with fresh pungent agave that fulfills a craving for both a clean mezcal and a wood-aged spirit.

LALOCURA

Lalocura is made by Eduardo Javier Ángeles Carreño ("Lalo") in Santa Catarina Minas. The name is a play on words, broken down into *Lalo* + *cura* or Lalo's remedy. Founded in 2014, Lalo brings with him the family legacy and training from his late father, master mezcalero Lorenzo Ángeles of Real Minero (page 196). He is humble and fiercely committed to tradition, sustainability, and passing on cultural wisdom. The ancestral mezcals he produces are widely recognized as some of the best available, and typically sell out fast due to the small-batch nature of his production. His mezcals are benchmark representations of the terroir of Santa Catarina Minas.

LALOCURA ESPADÍN

Lalo Ángeles, Santa Catarina Minas, Oaxaca
Espadín (**A. angustifolia**)

ABV: 49.4%
PRICE: $$$$

Refined, flavorful, and expressive. ■ Aromas are clean and inviting, with banana leaf, blueberries, and limestone. The flavor is bold with creamy tropical fruits, overripe mango, coffee, tangerine peel, and green chili spice that expands outward. The finish is soft, like silken velvet, and creamy with minerals.

LALOCURA CUISHE ESPADÍN

Lalo Ángeles, Santa Catarina Minas, Oaxaca
Cuishe, Espadín (**A. karwinskii, A. angustifolia**)

ABV: 50.4%
PRICE: $$$$

You can really take your time and get up close and personal with this mezcal. ■ Velvety aromas of soy sauce and musk draw you in as the aromas rise from the copita. Full bodied and rich, the savoriness flourishes on the palate, exploding with mushroom umami, brown-sugared orange peel, fermented bean paste, anise, vanilla, and cola.

LALOCURA PECHUGA

Lalo Ángeles, Santa Catarina Minas, Oaxaca

Tobasiche, Espadín (*A. karwinskii, A. angustifolia*)

ABV: 50.4%	Made with chicken, seasonal fruits, and botanicals. ■ Aromas of
PRICE: $$$$	oranges and herbal-laden citrus are plentiful on the nose. Pillowy in the

mouth with flavors of candied citrus rind, apples, tropical fruits, brown
sugar, and piña colada.

LALOCURA CUISHE 2017

Lalo Ángeles, Santa Catarina Minas, Oaxaca

Cuishe (*A. karwinskii*)

ABV: 47.7%	A flavorful option that is well suited to a pairing with salty
PRICE: $$$$	snacks. ■ Aromas are layered with different types of flowers like roses,

lavender, and orange blossom. The texture is supple and creamy, with toffee,
minty herbs, and roasted piña sweetness.

LALOCURA RESERVA ESPECIAL TEPEZTATE 2016

Lalo Ángeles, Santa Catarina Minas, Oaxaca

Tepeztate (*A. karwinskii*)

ABV: 48%	A favorite bottle from my personal collection that has aged
PRICE: n/a	beautifully. ■ Mineral-driven aromas with notes of sweet almond in the

background. Cilantro, mango, black pepper, spicy, earthy pine, and cedar are
all deep flavors that stretch into all corners of the palate. The texture is thick
and silken, getting more refined as it ages.

LALOCURA RESERVA ESPECIAL PULQUERO 30 AÑOS 2016

Lalo Ángeles, Santa Catarina Minas, Oaxaca

Pulquero

ABV: 47%	One of my most prized bottles from my personal collection, bittersweet
PRICE: n/a	to finish off the bottle. ■ Moss, strawberries, and juicy orange aromas are

soft and pretty. The texture is buttery smooth and rich. Flavors of pine needles
and sap, concentrated tropical fruits, cedar, and coffee all meld together
effortlessly. The flavors stay perfumed on the palate long after each sip.

LA LUNA MEZCAL

Salvador Chavez founded La Luna to celebrate his family's legacy in Michoacán, support local communities, and reconnect with his roots. His father grew up in Cotija—the town famous for its pungent, salty cheese—where he built a vinata that now produces mezcal for the brand. The brand also has a new custom-built vinata in Indaparapeo, and sources mezcal from Etucuaro. They now offer a wide variety of mezcals from Michoacán. While La Luna is at the beginning of its story, it has already had a positive impact in local communities and has been well received by agave-savvy industry and consumers internationally.

LA LUNA BRUTO

Hernan Hernandez Escot, Indaparapeo, Michoacán
Bruto (*A. inaequidens*), lot 34

ABV: 48.5%

PRICE: $$$$

A magical mezcal that makes you feel as good as it tastes. ▪ Immediately compelling, the aromas are deep and concentrated, showing bergamot, maple, and eucalyptus. There is a spicy-sweet earthiness, almost like sweet red onion, mixed with violets, clay, sage, and dried orange. The velveteen texture leaves the palate wanting more.

LA LUNA TEQUILANA

Hernan Hernandez Escot, Indaparapeo, Michoacán
Tequilana Blue Weber lot 26

ABV: 48.5%

PRICE: $$$

Made from the variety used to make tequila; a must-try for current or former tequila lovers. ▪ Lactic creaminess and tang are smooth and balanced aromas, mixing with daffodil and cucumber. In the mouth, the flavors begin with gentle spice, followed by sweet dragon fruit, green grapes, and a buttered coffee finish.

LA LUNA CHINO

Hernan Hernandez Escot, Indaparapeo, Michoacán

Chino (**A. cupreata**), lot 40

ABV: 48.5%

PRICE: $$$

A mezcal that shows off the delicate side of cupreata. ▪ Gentle aromas are mineral-driven with soft notes of white tea and lilies. The leathery texture reveals flavors of kiwi, asparagus, and dried plums. The finish is creamy with clay, minerals, and cardamom.

LA LUNA ENSEMBLE BRUTO + AZUL

Hernan Hernandez Escot, Indaparapeo, Michoacán

Bruto, Azul (**A. inaequidens**, Blue Weber), lot 29

ABV: 48.5%

PRICE: $$$

Rich earthy and fruity notes are enchanting. ▪ Fruity aromas show off berries and sugar plums, with supporting herbal overtones. Flavors of black tea, dried citrus, blueberries, and sweet spices all mix together effortlessly. Fresh acidity and a kiss of mint round out the finish.

MANSO SAHUAYO

Edgar Perez, Etucuaro, Michoacán

Manso Sahuayo (sp. not specified)

ABV: 48.5%

PRICE: $$$

A custard-like mezcal with tropical and peppery undertones. ▪ Green plantain and peppercorns are punchy and vibrant on the nose. The creamy texture pairs well with the custard-like flavors—papaya, sweet cream, and dried mango. The finish is soft, with long-lasting dried fruit flavors.

LAMATA

Luis Loya founded the brand Nación de las Verdes Matas as a way to feature uncertified agave spirits from northern Mexico, some coming from regions outside of the current denomination of origin. Lamata, formerly Amormata, is the exported collection. The brand seeks to offer historical tastes of these spirits, not changing them to fit into certification standards or in response to market trends. The batches are tiny, and each bottling is an extremely limited release.

LAMATA TEPEMETE DURANGO

Maximino Cruz, Mezquital, Durango
Tepemente (*A. angustifolia*)

ABV: 52%	A balanced high-alcohol mezcal with fluffy textures and flavors of
PRICE: $$$$	minerals and tropical fruits. ■ Mineral aromas of clay are earthy with

herbal and sweet green undertones. Spicy and fruity in the mouth. Tropical notes of pineapple and guava emerge alongside serrano, rosemary, and lemon zest flavors. The finish is soft, almost fluffy in texture.

LAMATA CENIZO DURANGO

Federico Cruz, Mezquital, Durango
Cenizo (*A. durangensis*)

ABV: 52.5%	Each sip is a symphony of flavors, instantly transportive to Durango
PRICE: $$$$	vinatas. ■ Super-fresh aromas of melons, grass, light smoke, and cucumbers

are bold and crisp. Juicy and a touch viscous on the palate. Earthy smoke, baked earth, red berry sweetness and tartness, and a gentle red chili spice create waves of flavor.

LAMATA NUEVO LEÓN

Jorge Torres, Santiago, Nuevo León

De Castilla (*A. americana*)

ABV: 49.4%	
PRICE: $$$$	

A unique and funky mezcal, combining fruit and earth similar to some *baijius*. ▪ Unique aromas of soursop, brine, and sherry are tangy and almost nutty and oxidized. The texture in the mouth is pillowy, contrasting with the earthy funk that permeates. Flavors of moss, autumn leaves, roses, and pineapple punctuate the finish.

LAMATA TAMAULIPAS

Jose Castellanos, Las Vírgenes, Tamaulipas

Amole, Asperrima, Americana (*A. univittata, A. asperrima, A. americana*)

ABV: 48%	
PRICE: $$$	

A cozy mezcal with soft textures and luxurious flavors. ▪ Elegant and refined even in the aromas. Notes of amber and musk are comforting and indulgent. The velvety texture holds layers of chocolate, green mango, roasted squash, and aji peppers. Floral, citrus, and piney notes linger on the finish.

LA MEDIDA

While relatively new outside of Mexico, La Medida has been in the works for decades, and it is well worth the wait. The brand was founded by Julián Gómez, one of the most knowledgeable people about the Oaxacan mezcal industry. His work stretches back forty years, before the contemporary industrialization of mezcal. The brand, co-operated with his son, draws on his longstanding relationships with mezcaleros and features high-quality single variety mezcals.

LA MEDIDA TEPEZTATE
Cipriano Hernandez, Ejutla, Oaxaca
Tepeztate (*A. marmorata*)

ABV: 47%
PRICE: $$$$

A delicious benchmark tepeztate. ■ Fresh aromas of cucumber, lilies, irises, sugarcane, and melon are focused and crisp. The texture is between chalky and silky, creating a lovely tension in the mouth. The flavors of juniper, sweet pea, and spicy ginger are bold and mouthcoating.

LA MEDIDA ESPADÍN
Celso Luis Santiago, San Pedro Quiatoni, Oaxaca
Espadín (*A. angustifolia*)

ABV: 48%
PRICE: $$$

Give this mezcal to people who think espadín is basic and watch their heads explode. ■ Roasted figs, salted orange, and smoked meats are rich aromas with both sweet and savory undertones. In the mouth, the flavors begin round and sweet, with roasted strawberries, fire-roasted red chili, toasted sesame, clay, and a dark chocolate finish.

LA MEDIDA MADRECUISHE

Antonio Cortés Aragón, Miahuatlán, Oaxaca

Madrecuishe (*A. karwinskii*)

ABV: 46%

PRICE: $$$$

A complex mezcal with infinite flavors to explore in each sip. ▪ Cooling herbal notes of aloe and tarragon match with sweet citrus and vanilla undertones. The flavor is spicy, with chili and warming baking spices filling the mouth. Tart minerals linger on the mouthwatering finish.

LA MEDIDA ARROQUEÑO

José Díaz Bustamante, Miahuatlán, Oaxaca

Arroqueño (*A. americana*)

ABV: 46%

PRICE: $$$$

A mezcal laden with earth and spice. ▪ Minerals and banana peel are soft and earthy aromas. The palate opens up with a hit of salt, followed by roasted asparagus, charred pineapple, and fresh pears. Green chili spice blankets the tongue as it softly morphs into a pillowy vanilla and limestone finish.

LA VENIA

Founded in 2009, this brand is owned and made by Celestino Cernas, Zapotec maestro mezcalero and magueyero in Santiago Matatlán, Oaxaca. He comes from a long line of mezcaleros and magueyeros, including his father, Zacarias, and his grandfather. Growing up in the palenque and among agaves, he brings a lifetime of experience to his craft, both in distilling and in growing agaves. Many of the artisanal mezcals are made from estate-grown agaves, all of which are capon. Celestino has nurseries for traditional wild varieties to implement semi-wild cultivation. Newly imported, it is an exciting addition to the international market. The mezcals are light in alcohol but still carry a balanced and focused flavor, which is distinct and varietally expressive in each bottle.

LA VENIA ESPADÍN

Celestino Cernas, Santiago Matatlán, Oaxaca
Espadín (*A. angustifolia*)

ABV: 40%
PRICE: n/a

Use this bottle to introduce people to mezcal. ■ The aromas are soft and fruity with green apple, green banana, and an earthy breeze. Crisp, cool, and refreshing, it would be easy to drink all night long.

LA VENIA TE LIMON

Celestino Cernas, Santiago Matatlán, Oaxaca
Espadín (*A. angustifolia*)

ABV: 40%
PRICE: n/a

A cheerful mezcal made with lemongrass in the last distillation. ■ The lemongrass comes through on the nose, spicy first, then fruity. Froot Loops–like flavors are citrusy, with melon, peach, and muscat grapes. Overall pillowy in the mouth, with a perfumed finish.

LA VENIA CUISHE

Celestino Cernas, Santiago Matatlán, Oaxaca

Cuishe (**A. karwinskii**)

ABV: 40%

PRICE: n/a

Vivacious and regal; share this one at parties. ■ Floral aromas of rose mix with dried berries, red plums, and candied hibiscus. Flavors of clay, orange zest, and raspberry are matched with vibrant red chili spice that makes the palate sing.

LA VENIA TOBALA

Celestino Cernas, Santiago Matatlán, Oaxaca

Tobala (**A. potatorum**)

ABV: 40%

PRICE: n/a

A refreshing mezcal with playful spice. ■ Minty, herbal, and creamy aromas are deceptively complex. The soft texture is punctuated with tingly spice, unleashing flavors of crushed rock minerality, dried eucalyptus, coriander seed, and cardamom.

LA VENIA TEPEZTATE

Celestino Cernas, Santiago Matatlán, Oaxaca

Tepeztate (**A. marmorata**)

ABV: 40%

PRICE: n/a

A tepeztate lover's mezcal, this is classic and clean. ■ Fresh and viny aromas are supported with notes of iris, dragon fruit, and ripe berries. In the mouth, the flavors turn roasted, with cacao nib, flan, and jalapeño pepper. A hint of chocolate brings out the earthy and rich coffee notes.

LEGENDARIO DOMINGO

Julian Saenger launched Legendario in 2014 as a celebration of the conviviality of Mexican culture. The name, which translates to Legendary Sunday, as well as the lively bottles that feature *papel picado* (colorful paper art), are designed to call in a celebratory moment to accompany the mezcals. Julian partners with artisanal producers from Oaxaca, Guerrero, Michoacán, and Durango to bottle small lots of mezcal. His philosophy is that each mezcal, even when produced by the same people, should be appreciated for its unique flavors, which vary from batch to batch.

LEGENDARIO DOMINGO ESPADÍN
Familia Valasco Cruz, San Luis del Río, Oaxaca
Espadín (*A. angustifolia*)

ABV: 48%

PRICE: $$

A delicious example of espadín. ■ Grapefruit oil, pine, and clove are strong aromas that hint at sweetness underneath the distinct earthiness. Roasted agave, light brown sugar, caramelized onions, and fire-roasted jalapeños are piquant and bold flavors. The finish has coffee and sweet spices.

LEGENDARIO DOMINGO ENSEMBLE
Familia Perez, Pie de la Mesa, Michoacán
Manso Sahuayo, Alto (sp. unclassified, *A. inaequidens*)

ABV: 47%

PRICE: $$$

Made by maestro José Valente Perez Rodriguez, one of the most celebrated maestros of his subregion in Michoacán. ■ Salty and earthy aromas show a touch of lactic funk. Deeply concentrated flavors coat the palate—malted milk balls, red chili, salted mango, and torched rosemary. The finish is creamy and herbal.

LEGENDARIO DOMINGO CUPREATA
Familia Obregón, Mazatlán, Guerrero
Papalote (*A. cupreata*)

ABV: 47%

PRICE: $$

A unique and superb mezcal full of fruit flavors. ■ Flowers and baking spices fill the nose. Light and airy in texture. Creamy vanilla, watermelon, pears, berries, plantain, and orange blossom cascade over the palate. Sweet herbs linger on the finish.

MEZCAL DE LEYENDAS

The precursor to this Mexican founded and owned brand was La Botica, a Mexico City–based mezcal bar that opened its doors in 2005. Today the brand is one of a few that represents so many different mezcal-producing regions, offering carefully selected spirits from maestros with generations of experience from each state. The brand is known for its commitment to category education and a strong line of core mezcals, along with special and limited releases. They remain one of the brands that continues to push the category forward while staying rooted in tradition, including a variety of regions and producing a mezcal using only solar power.

MEZCAL DE LEYENDAS ESPADÍN
Leo Hernández, San Baltazar Guelavila, Oaxaca
Espadín (*A. angustifolia*)

ABV: 50%
PRICE: $$$

A classic and delicious Oaxacan mezcal. Aromas of Meyer lemons and fresh pears are fruity and fresh. The rich oily texture complements the bright fruit on the palate, with a gentle smokiness woven throughout. No one flavor eclipses the other, creating a balanced flavor profile.

MEZCAL DE LEYENDAS TOBALA
Aarón Alva Sánchez, Huajuapan, Puebla
Tobala (*A. potatorum*)

ABV: 48%
PRICE: $$$

A mineral-focused spirit that expands over the palate. Peaches, clay, and cotton are soft aromas, along with earthy-sweet pineapple core. The minerality of tobala—a prized agave variety typical to Oaxaca and Puebla—takes over in the mouth, delivering broad strokes of granite, graphite, and limestone that coat the back of the tongue. The finish is refreshing with an earthy herbal lift.

MEZCAL DE LEYENDAS CENIZO

Ventura Gallegos, Nombre de Dios, Durango

Cenizo (**A. durangensis**)

ABV: 47%
PRICE: $$$

A delightful mezcal on its own or paired with anything chocolate or coffee. ▪ Mild and delicate aromas include vanilla custard and fresh farmers cheese. Soft and creamy in the mouth, the richness sinks into the tongue as flavors turn to roasted coffee and gently charred lemongrass.

MEZCAL DE LEYENDAS VERDE

Juan Jose Hernandez, Santa Isabel, San Luis Potosí

Verde (**A. salmiana**)

ABV: 45%
PRICE: $$

A medium funky mezcal that remains clean and precise in flavor. ▪ High-toned aromas are a touch funky with fermented notes, supported by juicy mango and honeydew. The flavors come alive on the palate, filling out with berries, woodsy herbs, and a chili spice–kissed finish.

MEZCAL DE LEYENDAS ANCHO

Oscar Obregón, Mazatlán, Guerrero

Ancho (**A. cupreata**)

ABV: 46%
PRICE: $$$

A very pretty mezcal, both delicate and bold in flavor. ▪ Aromas of pencil lead, roasted red bell peppers, and autumn leaves are crisp with substantial depth to them. Smooth and floral flavors float over the palate, with hints of rose and orange. The finish is creamy with a touch of mint and gentle smoke.

MEZCAL DE LEYENDAS VINATA SOLAR

Gerardo Ruelas, Nombre de Dios, Durango

Cenizo (**A. durangensis**)

ABV: 46%
PRICE: $$$

Made using a solar-powered still. ▪ Dried fruit aromas like banana and raisin are almost sherry-like. Gently sweet at first, the flavors turn spicy and floral with notes of honey, papaya, dried apricot, and vanilla.

LOS NAHUALES

Started in 1997 by twins in the restaurant business, Jaimé and Gustavo Muñoz, Los Danzantes was one of the first brands of traditional mezcal to make waves in the international market. In 2004, Ansley Coale, co-founder of California brandy distillery Germain Robin and founder of Craft Distillers, began importing the brand and continues to do so to this day. Also in 2004, chemist Karina Abad Rojas took over from the original distillery manager, Hector Vasquez de Abarca, to oversee an expansion as well as produce mezcal for the brand. Known as Los Danzantes in Mexico, Los Nahuales is identical except for the name, due to trademark issues.

LOS NAHUALES JOVEN

Hector Vasquez de Abarca, Karina Abad Rojas, Santiago Matatlán, Oaxaca
Espadín (*A. angustifolia*)

ABV: 47%
PRICE: $$

This shows off that espadín from Matatlán is diverse and capable of so much. ▪ Cut grass aromas are lively and fresh. Sweet like cactus fruit, honeydew, and other juicy green fruits. The spice is balanced with cacao and coffee notes, expanding the flavor throughout the palate. The finish is rounded and crisp.

THE LOST EXPLORER

A new brand of mezcal from David de Rothschild and Thor Björgólfsson in partnership with Infuse Spirits Group. The mezcals are crafted by the Ramos family in Oaxaca, who have an equity stake in the brand, and work with the typical varieties of the region. The brand places cultural and environmental sustainability front and center and is committed to working with three organizations that directly benefit Oaxacan communities in the areas of rainwater harvesting, gender equity, and artisan residencies and mentorship.

THE LOST EXPLORER ARTESANAL ESPADÍN 8 YEARS OLD
Fortino Ramos Florean, San Pablo Huixtepec, Oaxaca
Espadín (**A. angustifolia**)

ABV: 42%

PRICE: $$$

Light on agave character and full of fermentation flavors. ■ Overripe tropical fruits with a touch of funk characterize the aromas. In the mouth there is some sourness, followed quickly by intense earthy funk that is reminiscent of decaying leaves.

THE LOST EXPLORER ARTISANAL SALMIANA 12 YEARS OLD
Fortino Ramos Florean, San Pablo Huixtepec, Oaxaca
A. salmiana

ABV: 42%

PRICE: $$$$

A pungent and vegetal mezcal with a whisp of smokiness throughout. ■ The aromas are green and crisp, reminiscent of celery, parsley, and green pineapple fronds. The flavors have a charred note to them, offering tart and tangy grass, burnt orange, and soft minerals. The texture starts out dry and finishes mellow and soft.

LOS VECINOS DEL CAMPO

This brand launched in 2018 as a joint project between Casa San Matías, one of the oldest houses of tequila production, with parent company and international conglomerate Sazerac. Owner and CEO of Casa San Matías, Carmen Villareal, is at the helm of the project, which features mezcal made from a group of ten distillers across the Valles Centrales region of Oaxaca.

LOS VECINO DEL CAMPO ESPADÍN

Valles Centrales, Oaxaca

Espadín (*A. angustifolia*)

ABV: 45%

PRICE: $$

An easy-drinking mezcal with notes of roasted cacao. ■ Lightly smoked aromas of peaches, pineapple, and sunbaked earth. Mellow on the palate with notes of roasted chocolate, salt, grass, and hay. The finish is full of deeply roasted chocolate and coffee notes.

LOS VECINOS DEL CAMPO TOBALA

Valles Centrales, Oaxaca

Tobala (*A. potatorum*)

ABV: 46%

PRICE: $$$$

A fresh and floral tobala. ■ Soft aromas of flowers and earth and flavors of candied lemons, chamomile, capers, and aloe. The finish is creamy with sassafras, vanilla, and cloves.

LOS VECINOS DEL CAMPO ENSEMBLE NO.1

Valles Centrales, Oaxaca

Espadín, Barril, Madrecuishe (*A. angustifolia, A. karwinskii*)

ABV: 46%

PRICE: $

A well-made mezcal, with a flat finish. ■ Candied and sweet aromas like peach gummies. In the mouth, the flavors begin with roasted roots and carob before turning herbal with dried parsley and tarragon. A hint of cinnamon on the finish is warming.

MACURICHOS

Family owned and operated by the Martinez family, the palenque in Matatlán was founded in 1963 after generations of producing for other brands and at rented facilities. Today the company is run by maestro mezcalero Gonzalo and his brothers Pedro, Rafael, and Pablo, along with his nephew Valentin, who are grandsons and great-grandson of the original founder, for whom the brand is named. As the face of the brand, and someone who comes from a long lineage of mezcaleros, Gonzalo is outspoken about the need for cultural and environmental sustainability. They employ ancestral production methods, including distillation in clay pot stills.

MACURICHOS TEPEZTATE
Martinez Brothers, Santiago Matatlán, Oaxaca
Tepeztate (*A. marmorata*)

ABV: 50%
PRICE: $$$$

Pair this fresh and vibrant mezcal with winter cheese boards and chocolate desserts. ■ Berry and Persian cucumber aromas waft from the glass. The flavors skew sweet, with toffee and chocolate layers to be discovered underneath white strawberries and rosemary notes.

MACURICHOS ANCESTRAL TOBALA
Martinez Brothers, Santiago Matatlán, Oaxaca
Tobala (*A. potatorum*)

ABV: 48%
PRICE: $$$$

A classic tobala with layers of earthy sweetness. ■ Refreshing aromas are sweet and earthy with tender sprouts and juicy honeydew. Buttery in both texture and flavor, the nutty undertones blossom alongside deeply roasted green tea, and mint. The finish is clean with minerals and aloe.

MACURICHOS ENSEMBLE
Martinez Brothers, Santiago Matatlán, Oaxaca
Cirial, Madrecuishe, Barril, Bicuishe (*A. karwinskii*)

ABV: 53%
PRICE: $$$

A powerful yet refined and elegant mezcal. ■ Baking spices, leather, and smoked mango are warm and comforting aromas. The flavors are deep as they envelop the palate with roasted jalapeño, pineapple, hints of pine, and a floral finish.

MAL BIEN

Founded by US-based agave enthusiasts Ben Scott and Anthony Silas, this brand is a collection of uncertified mezcal from different producers and regions throughout Mexico. The cheeky branding is a nod to industry professionals and other agave enthusiasts who have come to associate their informally labeled bottles, with the ones that visitors bring home from Mexico in their suitcases and enjoy immediately while unpacking. Producer information and transparency are front and center in the branding, to the delight of their agave nerd customer base. Along with Neta (page 190), and Lalocura (page 166), Mal Bien is part of the Agave Mixtape subscription box, featuring limited release mini bottles from the three brands.

MAL BIEN MEZCAL ARTESANAL

Lucio Morales Lopez, San Dionisio Ocotepec, Oaxaca
Espadín (*A. angustifolia*)

ABV: 45.5%
PRICE: $$

An easy-drinking, great value mezcal. ▪ Smoked cherries and leather are crisp, autumnal aromas. The flavors start out with a hit of salt and tangy brine before developing into sweet earthy asparagus with a touch of piloncillo. Dried citrus and herbs linger on the finish.

MAL BIEN PAPALOTE

Ciro and Javier Barranca, Chilapa de Alvarez, Guerrero
Papalote (*A. cupreata*)

ABV: 47%
PRICE: $$$

A unique and dynamic sipping mezcal that is a treat to have in the glass. ▪ Honeyed aromas have an earthy backbone with dried firewood and carrot tops. The flavors burst onto the palate with tangy citrus and fresh acidity. The midpalate is ripe with jicama and sweet bell peppers, leading into a creamy vanilla and spice-kissed finish.

MAL BIEN QUIOTE DE ALTO

Isidro Rodriguez Montoya, Río de Parras, Michoacán

Alto (*A. inaequidens*)

ABV: 46.5%	Made exclusively from the quiote of the agave. A unique treat. ■
PRICE: $$$$	Fruity aromas are reminiscent of bubblegum, watermelon, and strawberry-flavored candy. The fruitiness is long lasting, accentuated with notes of berry rock candy and generous citrus-flecked spice that build on the palate after each sip.

MEZCALERO

This project from Ansley Coale of Craft Distillers, Los Nahuales (page 179), and Alipús (page 127) launched in 2011 as a way to celebrate the single-batch nature of mezcal. Ansley recognizes the deep relationship of Indigenous people with nature and specifically agave as a key element of artisanal mezcal, noting that making mezcal has profound cultural implications and goes way beyond simply running a still. Many of the producers featured have always made a living by selling their mezcal within their own communities. Releases are given a number and feature different producers from distinct regions, with all of the pertinent information on the bottle. Each one is a unique special bottling, and the brand is a curated tasting menu of artisanal mezcal.

MEZCALERO 23

Cosme and Cirilo Hernández, San Baltazar Guelavila, Oaxaca

Sierrudo (*A. americana*)

ABV: 46%	Smoky and fruity, with plenty of roasted agave character, a knockout
PRICE: n/a	example of Oaxacan mezcal. ■ Dried cherries, hardwood smoke, freshly tanned leather, and rosehips are punchy, vibrant aromas. Rich concentration of flavors is full of spearmint, red clay, toasted cacao, and smoked duck breast with a long cherry-almond finish.

MEZCALERO 25

Cosme and Cirilo Hernández, San Baltazar Guelavila, Oaxaca
Tobala (*A. potatorum*)

ABV: 47.5%
PRICE: $$$$

Yellow fruits abound in this well-balanced mezcal. ■ Aromas of lemons, lime zest, pastry cream, and orange bell peppers are bright and lively. Tropical fruit notes of guava and pineapple are accompanied by a suede-like texture. There are yellow plums and dried mango on the finish.

MEZCALERO SPECIAL BOTTLING 5

Rubén Solis Lozano, La Constancia, Durango
Cenizo, Espadín (*A. durangensis*, *A. angustifolia*)

ABV: 47%
PRICE: $$$$

Nice salinity; pair this stunner with oysters. ■ Savory aromas are meaty with sea spray and citrus. In the mouth, the earthiness is creamy and dried, with notes of hay, dried lily of the valley flowers, and crisp golden apple.

MEZCALOSFERA

This brand is the export arm of the renowned mezcaleria in Oaxaca Mezcaloteca, a play on words that combines mezcal and the Spanish word for library, *biblioteca*. As the name suggests, it is a veritable library and educational center for all things mezcal. With deep connections throughout the world of producers, and committed to a labor of love, owner Sylvia Philion sources small batches of prized agave distillates for the limited releases. The label offers detailed information about every batch.

MEZCALOSFERA ENSEMBLE
Emanuel Ramos, Miahuatlán, Oaxaca
Madrecuishe, Bicuishe, Espadín (*A. karwinskii*, *A. karwinskii*, *A. angustifolia*)

ABV: 47.61%

PRICE: $$$$

Made by Emanuel Ramos (the son of renowned maestro Victor Ramos), who also produces mezcal for Gusto Histórico (page 161) and Mal Bien (page 183). ■ Bold aromas of green vines, woodsy herbs, and rich coffee, followed by explosive flavors of red chili, raspberry cream, lilies, and orange blossom. Hearty baked earth notes lend a touch of rustic leatheriness to the finish amid the candied red fruit notes.

MEZONTE

Mezonte is a Guadalajara-based non-governmental organization founded by Pedro Jimenez Gurria and is imported in partnership with David Suro of Siembra Valles (page 113), and Siembra Azul (page 112). Mezonte describes itself as an organization that promotes, preserves, and supports traditional agave spirits and the communities that make them, and they lead by example with radical business transparency. Mezonte works with producers from different regions, with a focus on Michoacán and Jalisco. In addition to their internationally available bottlings, there is an educational tasting room in Guadalajara. The small batches are consistently some of the best agave spirits available anywhere inside or outside of Mexico.

MEZONTE CANDIDO

Candido Romero, Loma de Guadalupe, Jalisco
Ixtero Amarillo (*A. maximiliana*)

ABV: 45%
PRICE: $$$$

This 77-liter micro batch is out of this world good, and it will only get better in the bottle. ■ Melon husk, pear, bloomy rind cheese, and sweet malt are fragrantly smooth. Nectar-like, the full body is dripping with honeyed fruits, tobacco, and smoked cherry. Warm spices, piney freshness, and sunbaked earth unfold, leaving behind a trail of shimmering light spice.

MEZONTE TEPE

Aciano Mendoza, Tepehuano
Cenizo (*A. shrevei*)

ABV: 51%
PRICE: $$$$

From an Indigenous Tepehuano community in a region between Jalisco, Nayarit, and Durango. ■ Fennel, coriander, pine, and a touch of acetones are pungent aromas. The flavor ping-pongs between metallic and floral. Mineral and spruce tip notes are bold. The flavors continue to open up in the glass as it breathes.

MEZONTE MICHOACÁN

Jorge Perez, Río de Parras, Michoacán

Alto (*A. inaequidens*)

ABV: 54.5%

PRICE: $$$$

Distilled with guavas, this mezcal is from an iconic producer. ■ The aromas are complex and alluring, gently sweet and fruity, with background forest notes. The peachy, fruity, and floral flavors of the guava are gentle, as a slow creeping spice blankets the tongue. The finish is silken with lemon balm. Delicious.

MEZONTE CENIZO 21 AÑOS

Hildegardo Joya, Cabo Corrientes, Jalisco

Cenizo

ABV: 50%

PRICE: n/a

This 2010 lot was fermented for thirty days, and produced just 100 liters. ■ Smells like bubbling mac and cheese with a crust, pine, and red chili. The flavors radiate out from a peppery core. Cinnamon flan and tropical fruits turn into roasted cacao, chicories, and dried mint. The texture is rich and almost waxy. The flavors melt into the tongue, lingering after the sip is long gone.

MONTELOBOS

Founded by industry giant and organic chemist Ivan Saldaña, Montelobos launched in 2012 and has been nothing short of a success story. Today, the brand has its own dedicated palenque, run by maestro mezcalero Abel Lopez. Casa Lumbre became the umbrella company for Montelobos, along with Ancho Reyes chili liqueurs, Abasolo whisky, and Ojo de Tigre mezcal. In 2019, international conglomerate Campari bought a majority stake in Montelobos, with Casa Lumbre owning the remaining 49%. While Campari controls all of the marketing and sales, Montelobos's parent company, Casa Lumbre, maintains control over the product. Their line has expanded to include expressions from Puebla in addition to Oaxaca.

MONTELOBOS ESPADÍN
Abel Lopez, Santiago Matatlán, Oaxaca
Espadín (*A. angustifolia*)

ABV: 43.2%

PRICE: $$

A light mezcal with soft edges that mixes well into cocktails and goes down easy. ■ Aromas are mild, with suggestions of herbs and honeysuckle. It starts out tart and bright in the mouth, with tangerine, light smoke, and freshly cut grass. Green bell peppers and poblano-like spice give way to softer flavors of marshmallow and hay.

MONTELOBOS TOBALA
Aarón Alva Sánchez, San Nicolás Huajuapan, Puebla
Tobala (*A. potatorum*)

ABV: 46.8%

PRICE: $$$

A mineral-driven mezcal. ■ Very mild aromatically. Red chili paste, clay, and green cactus fruit open on the palate, followed by citrus peel and mace. Minerality characterizes the finish.

NETA

Neta was founded by a group of three young creatives with diverse backgrounds—Niki Nakazawa, Max Rosenstock, and Yuseki Murayama—all united by a common love and appreciation for mezcal and the communities that produce it. The brand features individual producers as well as a co-op of producers from the renowned Oaxacan subregion of Miahuatlán, known for its high-quality traditionally made spirits. While a relative newcomer to the craft mezcal scene, their limited small batches can be found at the hottest bars and restaurants, and in agave-savvy bottle shops.

NETA ENSEMBLE 2012
Candido G Cruz, Miahuatlán, Oaxaca
Espadín, Bicuishe (*A. angustifolia*, *A. karwinskii*)

ABV: 46%
PRICE: $$$$

Lusciously thick flavors and textures here. ▪ Rich and velvety aromas include musk, plums, and cinnamon basil. The deep concentration translates to the mouth with flavors of cactus fruit, pomegranate molasses, and cinnamon stick.

NETA ESPADÍN 2017
Candido G Cruz, Miahuatlán, Oaxaca
Espadín (*A. angustifolia*)

ABV: 47%
PRICE: $$$$

Well-balanced flavors show off the diversity that distilled agave offers. ▪ Pineapple jam, kiwi, and lemon balm are sweet, tart, and earthy on the nose. Impeccable balance on the palate, the silky texture unfurls offering notes of Meyer lemon, green apple, and orange blossom.

NETA ENSEMBLE 2020
Hermógenes Vasquez, Miahuatlán, Oaxaca
Barril, Mexicano (*A. karwinskii*, *A. rhodacantha*)

ABV: 47.5%
PRICE: $$$$

Slightly lactic and funky, this mezcal is ripe with fermentation notes. ▪ Aromas of soursop and slight lactic notes are clean with just a whisper of funk. The flavors begin sweet with rock sugar, then turn umami-rich with dried meat. The finish is kissed with spice and subtle smoke.

NOBLE COYOTE

Oaxacan-born evolutionary biologist Bernardo Sada launched Noble Coyote in 2013 and operates the brand along with Eleazar Brena, Oaxacan agronomist and professor, and Brena's father, fifth-generation mezcalero Marcos Brena. They are leaders who support seed saving and the practice of semi-wild cultivation in their communities with the goal of letting over-harvested ancestral landscapes heal. Their mezcals offer a site-specific taste, born from the traditional practices of the towns they come from.

NOBLE COYOTE TOBALA

Eleazar and Marcos Brena, San Luis Amatlán, Oaxaca
Tobala (*A. potatorum*)

ABV: 48%
PRICE: $$$

A tart and lactic tobala. ■ Red fruits, leather, and roasted pineapple aromas, followed by tart flavors raspberry and then a lactic creaminess and a touch of funk and sour cream. The earthy potato finish is clean.

NOBLE COYOTE JABALÍ

Eleazar and Marcos Brena, Santiago Matatlán, Oaxaca
Jabalí (*A. convalis*)

ABV: 48%
PRICE: $$$$

A spicy and indulgently silky mezcal. ■ Spicy from the get-go, aromas of clove and anise leap from the copita. The rich texture cascades over the palate with notes of pine, apple and pear skin, almonds, and lilies. A soft sweetness and richness persist after each sip.

NUESTRA SOLEDAD

Owned and operated by Casa Cortés along with El Jolgorio (page 155), Nuestra Soledad features regionally specific espadín mezcals from a variety of producers. The entire brand is an exercise in Oaxacan terroir, highlighting the difference in flavors and technique from the producers of distinct subregions.

NUESTRA SOLEDAD MIAHUATLÁN
Pedro Vásquez, Miahuatlán, Oaxaca
Espadín (*A. angustifolia*)

ABV: 49%
PRICE: $$

A good value mezcal with terroir expressive flavors. ▪ Peaches, baked and preserved. White pepper and banana custard. Soft and buttery texture plays into the lightly caramelized and pudding-like flavors.

NUESTRA SOLEDAD ZOQUITLÁN
Ignacio Parada, Zoquitlán, Oaxaca
Espadín (*A. angustifolia*)

ABV: 48%
PRICE: $$

A great value mezcal made by Don Chucho, a locally renowned maestro. ▪ Meaty aromas with peppers and basil. The flavors are full and round, full of eucalyptus, tangerine, and green coffee.

ORIGEN RAÍZ

Origen Raíz uniquely combines the traditions and agaves of two regions: Oaxaca and Durango. The brand is a joint project between the renowned Oaxacan maestro Valentin Cortés and his son Asis and the Saravia family of Durango. The flagship Durango vinata uses Oaxacan techniques like a horse-drawn tahona for crushing and aboveground wooden fermentation tanks. The brand recently expanded to include offerings from more regions of Durango by various family producers. They are one of the few widely available brands from Durango that seek to represent the state's diversity. The Oaxacan-based production is out of Guardianes del Mezcal, the same palenque as the father and son's other brand, Dixeebe (page 148).

ORIGEN RAÍZ CHACALEÑO
Carlos Ángulo Ríos, Topia, Durango
Chacaleño (**A. angustifolia**), 2nd edition

ABV: 48%
PRICE: $$$

Distilled in a remote region with a hyper-local subvariety of angustifolia, this rare mezcal is a gem. ■ Notes of mixed berries, muscat grapes, and minerals are subtle yet aromatically clear and focused. The texture is rich with some weighty oiliness, enhancing the earthy pine and dried grass flavors. Charred herbs and pineapple husk on the finish are layered with caramel and warm spices.

ORIGEN RAÍZ PECHUGA VENADO
Valentin Cortés, Tuitán, Durango
Cenizo (**A. durangensis**), 3rd edition

ABV: 50%
PRICE: $$$$

Distilled with deer meat and seasonal fruits, this is rich and satisfying. ■ Plums and smoked meat are vibrant and inviting aromas. Rich and spiced flavors of cinnamon, marigold, dark chocolate, and blood orange are velvety, with deep caramelized brown sugar on the finish.

ORIGEN RAÍZ CENIZO

Ignacio Grijalva, Tuitán, Durango

Cenizo (*A. durangensis*), 20th edition

ABV: 48%

PRICE: $$$

The flagship mezcal of the brand made from the most common local variety of agave. ■ Sweet and gently smoky aromas are ripe with red fruits, apple blossom, and fresh green clover. In the mouth, the texture starts smooth and silky with rounded notes of pear, sea salt, and green coffee. Brash spice fills in the body as the texture turns dusty, with toasted complexity on the finish.

PIERDE ALMAS

One of the first artisanal mezcal brands to hit shelves a decade ago, before the explosive mezcal boom of the last few years, Pierde Almas was created by artist Jonathan Barbieri. Partnering with traditional producers, the brand features high-alcohol mezcals from wild and semi-wild local varieties. Barbieri was the first to distill and bring to market a gin-like mezcal using nine classic gin botanicals. The brand was purchased by international conglomerate Diageo in 2018, which has brought about significant changes.

PIERDE ALMAS TEPEXTATE

Gregorio Velasco/Rodolfo Hernandez, San Juan del Río/San Luis del Río, Oaxaca

Tepextate (*A. marmorata*), lot PAZ-801

ABV: 55%

PRICE: $$$$

Rich, full, and spicy, this is a benchmark tepeztate. ■ A smoky aroma is supported with minerals, meaty undertones, and red fruit notes. In the mouth, the concentrated flavors of red cactus fruit, watermelon rind, campfire, and rich lactic notes evolve into charred pineapple. The finish is rich with dried chili powder and citrus acidity.

RAYO SECO

Launched in 2017, Rayo Seco is a new-to-market brand with mezcal from Guerrero and Durango. Owned by Edgar Salazar and his wife, Carolina Mora, they work with different producers that are third- and fourth-generation mezcaleros, including Edgar's uncle, to source traditionally made mezcals. The small-batch mezcals are an addition to the limited offerings from Guerrero, a state that has historically been difficult to source mezcal from because of sociopolitical turmoil.

RAYO SECO CUPREATA ANCESTRAL
Margarito López Flores, Chichihualco, Guerrero
Cupreata

ABV: 48.5%	A bold and full-flavored mezcal, expressive of its terroir. ◼ Pungent aromas of tomato and herbs, celery, and iris blossoms. It begins earthy in the mouth with a gentle blanket of green spice. Red fleshy fruits like plums and watermelon turn to coffee and ash on the finish.
PRICE: n/a	

REAL MINERO

This iconic brand from Santa Caterina Minas is the work of the well-known Ángeles Carreño family. Formerly made by the great late Don Lorenzo, his son Edgar now manages production while his daughter Graciela promotes the brand as an active leader in the Oaxacan mezcal community. Graciela's efforts have made waves in the local and international industry, pioneering Indigenous women's leadership in the contemporary mezcal scene. The brand is also a pioneer of agave nurseries for species preservation, biodiversity, and sustainability. Committed to tradition, the ancestral mezcals offer a regionally specific taste of the production techniques and agave varieties from Santa Caterina Minas.

REAL MINERO ESPADÍN Y LARGO
Espadín, Largo Carreño, Santa Catarina Minas, Oaxaca
Espadín, Largo (*A. angustifolia*, *A. karwinskii*)

ABV: 51.6%
PRICE: $$$$

This is a good choice for those looking for complex, rather than smoky, mezcal. ■ Soft and creamy clay aromas gently waft up from the copita. Inky flavors saturate the palate with crisp pear, red plums, and chocolate. Roasted asparagus, herbs, and a light floral quality are layered within the rich silken texture.

REAL MINERO BECUELA
Edgar Ángeles Carreño, Santa Catarina Minas, Oaxaca
Becuela (*A. marmorata*)

ABV: 48%
PRICE: $$$$

Distilled in 2019 and aged in glass for eighteen months, only forty-five bottles of this stellar mezcal were produced. ■ Earthy aromas are slightly spicy, reminiscent of a fully loaded elote, or Mexican street corn. The texture is wine-like, silky with some tannic dryness. Toasted coffee, caramelized shallot, and dried lavender are graceful on the finish.

REAL MINERO MARTEÑO

Edgar Ángeles Carreño, Santa Catarina Minas, Oaxaca
Marteño (**A. karwinskii**)

ABV: 52%

PRICE: $$$$

The high alcohol balances easily with the layered flavors. ▪ Dry on the nose and on the palate. Dried chile de arbol and serrano are chalky, with background notes of pine and baked earth. Clay and sweetgrass dust round out the finish.

REAL MINERO LARGO

Edgar Ángeles Carreño, Santa Catarina Minas, Oaxaca
Largo (**A. karwinskii**)

ABV: 50.6%

PRICE: $$$$

Agave characteristics are front and center, with notes from the clay supporting the overall flavor. ▪ Sweet baking spices, cola, and vanilla are warm aromas, if a bit subtle. Caramelized delicata squash, nasturtium flowers, and papaya seed are also sweet and spicy flavors. The clay flavors bind with notes of coffee and sweet tobacco on the finish.

REAL MINERO BARRIL

Edgar Ángeles Carreño, Santa Catarina Minas, Oaxaca
Barril (**A. karwinskii**)

ABV: 50.7%

PRICE: $$$$

This one is for the agave geeks to sip on and gush over. ▪ Banana and Nilla Wafers are comforting aromas. Ripe custard apple, guava, banana leaf, and coffee are tropical flavors. A chalky texture and mild habanero heat add another dimension.

REY CAMPERO

Hailing from the small village of Candelaria Yegolé within the Zoquitlán municipality of the Sierra Sur of Oaxaca, this is a producer-owned family collective with Romulo Sanchez Parada at the helm. The family has invested in nurseries for all types of local agave varieties, including some that were not typically cultivated before. They are known for traditional flavors, and the expertise of multiple generations is evident in their small batch releases.

REY CAMPERO TEPEZTATE PULQUERO
Romulo Sanchez Parada, Zoquitlán, Oaxaca
Tepeztate, Pulquero (**A. marmorata, A. atrovirens**), October 2017

ABV: 49%
PRICE: $$$$

A wine lover's dream; pair this with silky stews. ■ Aromas of baking spices, fresh pine, and freshly split jalapeño are clean and zesty. Citrusy, rich, velvety texture and dry wine-like tannins with flavors of chipotle, dried orange, and caramel are balanced and *en su punto*, or "at its perfect point."

REY CAMPERO MEXICANO
Romulo Sanchez Parada, Zoquitlán, Oaxaca
Mexicano (**A. rhodacantha**), March 2018

ABV: 48%
PRICE: $$$

A triumph of a mezcal that tastes great and lifts the spirits. ■ Tropical piña colada aromas are sweet and caramelized. The indulgent aromas don't lie: it's just as sweet, creamy, fruity, and nutty as you want it to be.

REY CAMPERO TEPEXTATE
Romulo Sanchez Parada, Zoquitlán, Oaxaca
Tepeztate (**A. marmorata**), March 2017

ABV: 48.7%
PRICE: $$$$

A distinctive mezcal; pair with flourless chocolate cake and espresso. ■ Green bean aromas are vegetal, sweet, and fresh. The flavors coat the mouth with spicy citrus, dusty tobacco, and charred onion.

SACRO IMPERIO

Sacro Imperio is one of the many brands made by Manuel Simental and his family, well known in Durango as a true master of his craft. The brand was founded under the name Mezcal Fundadores in 2015 by Alan Fernando García Flores, and is co-owned by Ricardo Aviles Lopez. In 2016, the name changed to Sacro Imperio. It has been imported to the United States by the Lizarraga Company since 2019 and quickly landed on the radars of mezcal lovers. Production uses regionally traditional in-ground fermentation tanks and a wooden hat still. Across the board, the flavor profile features the wild-grown agaves and downplays the smoke. Anything from Manuel Simental is fantastic, and Sacro Imperio is no exception.

SACRO IMPERIO CENIZO
Manuel Simental, Nombre de Dios, Durango
Cenizo (*A. durangensis*)

ABV: 48%

PRICE: $$

A tasty mezcal that is easy to love for both novices and experienced drinkers. ■ The earthy aromas show notes of lemon balm and minerals. Chalky mineral flavors fill the mouth, with hints of melon, pea shoots, and basil. The finish is smooth, with a touch of chocolate.

SAN COSME

Three childhood friends who wanted to highlight their beloved Mexican culture founded San Cosme in 2010. Their mezcals were originally produced for the German market, but are now available all over Europe, the United States, and beyond. The brand is named after the patron saint of medicine, San Cosmas.

SAN COSME JOVEN
Wilfrido Hernandez, Santiago Matatlán, Oaxaca
Espadín (**A. angustifolia**)

ABV: 40%	Not much flavor here. ■ Very subtle aromatically, with hints of agave
PRICE: $$	and smoke. Equally subtle in flavor, there are background notes of spice, chocolate, and dried citrus. The finish is mildly herbal.

SOMBRA

Sombra, launched in 2008, was among the first wave of widely available mezcals in the international market. The espadín-based mezcal is a standard in cocktail programs at agave-focused bars around the world. Their unique sustainability efforts include solar-powered crushing and manufacturing adobe bricks from the materials left over after production. The Oaxaca-based brand was founded by wine industry veteran Richard Betts. In 2020 Davos Brands, then the parent company of the brand, was acquired by international conglomerate Diageo.

SOMBRA JOVEN
Isaias Martinez Juan, San Juan del Río/San Luis del Río, Oaxaca
Espadín (**A. angustifolia**)

ABV: 45%	An easy-drinking mezcal with bold flavors that stand up in
PRICE: $	cocktails. ■ Smoke and ginger are inviting aromas. The flavors show piloncillo, charred pineapple husk, red chili, and clay.

TLAMATI

Tlamati is a Nahuatl word that translates to "to know" or "to feel," which speaks to the brand's championing of the Indigenous culture behind agave spirits. The Puebla-based brand was founded in 2018 by a group of five friends, following a decade of working with the producers and adopting a co-op model that ensures producers directly benefit from the success of the brand. They are one of the only Puebla-focused artisanal brands available internationally, showcasing a variety of local agave varieties, no doubt leading the way for more brands to follow suit shortly.

TLAMATI ESPADILLA
Balbino and Sergio Salas, San Miguel Atlapulco, Puebla
Espadilla (*A. angustifolia*)

ABV: 49%
PRICE: $$$$

Bold, focused flavors are easily enjoyable from this terroir-focused spirit. ▪ Cheesy lactic notes are subdued, with roasted agave, pineapple frond, and a hint of smoke on the nose. The leathery texture adds complexity to the mix of sweet, roasted, and earthy flavors. Notes of clay, vanilla, and toasted buckwheat persist on the finish.

TLAMATI PAPALOMETL
Balbino and Sergio Salas, San Miguel Atlapulco, Puebla
Papalometl (*A. potatorum*)

ABV: 46.7%
PRICE: $$$$

A unique mix of sweet and spicy flavors with a full body and texture. ▪ Aromatically mild, the charm of this mezcal is in the flavor. Full-bodied spicy notes show off ginger, epazote, crisp apple, and a touch of caramel. A mineral, peachy, and vanilla-kissed finish is leathery and long.

TOSBA

Tosba comes to us from cousins Edgar González Ramírez and Elisandro González Molina, who immigrated to the US like many Oaxacans, searching for economic opportunities. In 1999, full of entrepreneurial spirit and concerned about the mass migration from their hometown, they decided to go back to their Oaxacan mountain village of San Cristóbal Lachirioag and start a mezcal brand. Edgar began the operation by planting agave on the family land and then learned how to distill. Tosba's success is an inspiring story of reconnection with nature, community, and culture. The mezcals are known as some of the best available and feature unique flavors due to the climate and biodiversity of the region, where agaves grow among coffee, fruit trees, and sugar cane. Recently, the brand has expanded to include mezcal produced from agaves sourced from Durango in addition to their own local varieties. They also produce Rum Dakabend from a local sugarcane.

TOSBA ESPADÍN
Edgar González, San Cristóbal Lachirioag, Oaxaca
Espadín (*A. angustifolia*)

ABV: 45.4%
PRICE: $$

A well-balanced mezcal with bright and rich flavors. ■ Aromas are complex with pineapple and pineapple husk, peppery spices, and clay. In the mouth, the flavors play between bright green fruits and roasted cacao nib.

TOSBA WARASH
Edgar González, San Cristóbal Lachirioag, Oaxaca
Warash (sp. unclassified)

ABV: 50.65%
PRICE: $$

Made from a unique local variety, a rare treat. ■ The flavors and aromas are zesty with lime and other citrus, spicy chilies, and a meaty body. The gentle smoke enhances the fruit notes by contrast, creating a balanced and unique flavor profile.

TOSBA TEPEXTATE

Edgar González, San Cristóbal Lachirioag, Oaxaca

Tepextate (*A. marmorata*)

ABV: 47.38%

PRICE: $$$$

An absolute pleasure to sip. ▪ Fruity aromas show mineral undertones and berry tartness. In the mouth, the minerals are front and center, with supporting flavors of raspberries, plantain, and cocoa powder.

TOSBA TOBALA

Edgar González, San Cristóbal Lachirioag, Oaxaca

Tobala (*A. potatorum*)

ABV: 48%

PRICE: $$$$

A tasty tobala with sweet tropical undertones. ▪ Aromas are clean with herbal freshness. The flavors are balanced between sweet and caramelized with light and airy earthiness. Notes of pineapple preserves, basil, and green tea are evenly layered.

TOSBA PECHUGA

Edgar González, San Cristóbal Lachirioag, Oaxaca

Espadín (*A. angustifolia*)

ABV: 47.35%

PRICE: $$$$

A benchmark pechuga, it's hard to imagine a better bottle to pour for special celebrations. ▪ Immediately rich aromas of dried fruits are figgy and concentrated. In the mouth, the flavors of citrus, raisins, dried cherries, and smoked caramel are intertwined on a buttery rich texture.

UNION

Launched in 2011, the name of the brand is also their operations model, based on a union of mezcal producers from Oaxaca. They use a unique solera system, or fractional blending, to achieve consistency across batches that features individual lots from ten unique producers. In 2017, international conglomerate Diageo made a distribution deal with the brand, and in 2021 they acquired the parent company of Union.

UNION JOVEN

San Baltazar Guelavila, Oaxaca

Espadín, Cirial, Barril (*A. angustifolia*, *A. karwinskii*)

ABV: 40%

PRICE: $

Nice flavors, though the low alcohol keeps them being fully expressed. ▪ Aromas of baked earth and creamy clay remain uplifted and airy. Once in the mouth, the flavors build until reaching a crescendo of rich chocolate, roasted greens, and leather. The flavors fade quickly from the palate.

VAGO

The seed of this brand was planted when US-born and raised Judah Kuper fell ill while living in Oaxaca, then fell in love with his nurse and future wife, Valentina. She is the daughter of Aquilino Garcia Lopez, one of the most celebrated mezcaleros. By 2013, Judah and his new father-in-law started exporting. Sadly, Aquilino passed away in 2020, but the brand had already expanded to include other family and friends who also produce traditional mezcal. The brand has earned a reputation for excellent quality and value, and today represents four families, including the sons of Aquilino. In 2018, Vago entered into partnership with Samson and Surrey, a company started by ex-Bacardi executives that invests in high-end spirits; no changes to production or production management have occurred due to the partnership.

VAGO ELOTE

Hijos de Aquilino Garcia López, Candelaria Yegolé, Oaxaca
Espadín (*A. angustifolia*)

ABV: 50%
PRICE: $$

The elegant flavors of family-grown heirloom corn shine through. ■ Soft corn notes show through on the aromas along with hay and dried lemon peel. Incredibly round and smooth, flavors of tortillas, pineapple husk, and roasted tomatillo are bright and earthy.

VAGO ESPADÍN JB

Joel Barriga, Hacienda Tapanala, Oaxaca
Espadín (*A. angustifolia*)

ABV: 50%
PRICE: $$$

There are layers of flavor to uncover in each sip. ■ Buttery pie crust, condensed milk, and grilled mushrooms are pungent on the nose. Bright acidity open on the palate, with notes of juicy orange, clay, limestone, and lemon leaf.

VAGO ENSAMBLE EN BARRO

Salomón Rey Rodriguez, Sola de Vega, Oaxaca

Espadín, Tepeztate (**A. angustifolia, A. marmorata**)

ABV: 48.5%	An iconic mezcal from an iconic maestro. ▪ Roasted plums, violets, and
PRICE: $$$	plantains are deep aromas. Flavors of spearmint are refreshing, mixed with

mineral-rich soil, pears, and aromatic green grapes. A white pepper spice gently builds on the palate, tingling long after each sip.

VAGO ESPADÍN EJ

Emigdio Jarquín, Miahuatlán, Oaxaca

Espadín (**A. angustifolia**)

ABV: 50%	Spicy and balanced, a good example of artisanal
PRICE: $$$	mezcal. ▪ Fermentation notes are clean and aromatic, showing off pickled

fruits and brine. The flavors are bold, washing over the palate with jalapeño, rye, caramelized onion, and salted butter.

VAGO MADRECUIXE

Emigdio Jarquín, Miahuatlán, Oaxaca

Madrecuixe (**A. karwinskii**)

ABV: 50%	A sturdy mezcal with flavors that extend well beyond
PRICE: $$$	smokiness. ▪ Melons and clay are subtle aromas. The flavors start off with

ripe citrus, mixed chilies, and rosemary. Not overly smoky, a pleasant leathery flavor and texture add depth to the finish.

WAHAKA

The core line of mezcal is made by fifth-generation Zapotec maestro mezcalero Alberto Morales in San Dionisio Ocotepec, Oaxaca. The brand is a partnership between a group of friends from Mexico City and Morales, and hinges on the Morales family's commitment to the artisanal production that has been passed down through their family lineage. They offer a wide variety of mezcals, including special releases like the new gin-esque Botanika, and recently launched a new cocktail and all-purpose mezcal, El Güel, which comes from a small artisanal cooperative of young, upcoming producers from the same village. As part of the central philosophy of keeping traditions alive, they are active in promoting and practicing both cultural and environmental sustainability.

WAHAKA BOTANIKO
Alberto Morales Mendez, San Dionisio Ocotepec, Oaxaca
Espadín (*A. angustifolia*)

ABV: 45%
PRICE: $$$

Infused in the last distillation with botanicals, similar to gin. Crisp herbs and zesty citrus aromas are refreshing. The flavors are equally zippy, with lavender, apples, clove, and paprika. The finish is ripe with cardamom.

WAHAKA TOBALA
Alberto Morales Mendez, San Dionisio Ocotepec, Oaxaca
Tobala (*A. potatorum*)

ABV: 42%
PRICE: $$$

Ultra smooth, floral, and earthy. Citrus and taffy notes have underlying aromas of copper and granite. The flavors are floral in the mouth, showing honeysuckle and lily of the valley alongside lime zest and more minerals. Baked artichoke lingers on the soft finish.

WAHAKA MADRECUISHE

Alberto Morales Mendez, San Dionisio Ocotepec, Oaxaca

Madrecuishe (*A. karwinskii*)

ABV: 42%

PRICE: $$$

A low-alcohol but tasty example of madrecuishe. ■ Purple flowers, blackberries, and grilled pineapple are pretty aromas. Inky flavors of plum, cherries, and chocolate are lightly roasted. Charred red bell pepper is sweet and earthy on the finish.

WAHAKA ABOCADO CON GUSANO

Alberto Morales Mendez, San Dionisio Ocotepec, Oaxaca

Espadín (*A. angustifolia*)

ABV: 40%

PRICE: $$

Infused with a maguey worm, each bottle comes with its own gusano. ■ There is a slight amber tinge to the mezcal. The aromas are rich with the earthiness of the gusano de maguey. Flavors like hay and roasted chestnuts permeate the palate, blending with roasted pineapple notes.

EL GÜEL

Alberto Morales Mendez, San Dionisio Ocotepec, Oaxaca

Espadín (*A. angustifolia*)

ABV: 42%

PRICE: $$

Aptly designed as an all-purpose cocktail mezcal. ■ Smoky aromas are mild, with green pineapple husk. Light on the palate, with flavors of green peach, asparagus, and baked apricot. Soft minerality and just a touch of spice round out the finish.

ZINACANTÁN

Zinacantán is a Nahuatl word that translates to "land of bats," which highlights this brand's commitment to sustainability. Owner and master distiller Fabiola Torres Monfil comes from a fourth-generation family of mezcal and pulque producers, and after five years working full-time in mezcal, she inaugurated her new fabrica in 2020. Her nurseries are full of baby agaves started from seed and grown organically, fertilized with repurposed and treated by-products from previous batches, and planted in semi-wild cultivation using a proprietary anti-erosion system. A portion of the agaves are left to flower for the bats and eventually seed, increasing the biodiversity of agave species. The mezcals are delicious, and Zinacantán is one of the newly available brands in the United States pioneering the contemporary wave of mezcal from Puebla.

ZINACANTÁN ESPADÍN 2017

Fabiola Torres Monfil, San Diego La Meza Tochimiltzingo, Puebla
Espadín (*A. angustifolia*)

ABV: 50%
PRICE: n/a

Layers of flavor range from fruit to floral to roasted nuts. ▪ The nose is rich with red chilies, daffodils, pears, and chocolate. In the mouth, flavors are citrusy with a piquant serrano backbone, sweet peaches, and strawberries, and a fruity coffee finish.

ZINACANTÁN PECHUGA 2019

Fabiola Torres Monfil, San Diego La Meza Tochimiltzingo, Puebla
Espadín (*A. angustifolia*)

ABV: 49%
PRICE: n/a

A soft and flavorful mole pechuga. ▪ The aromas are of mole, with dried chilies, chocolate, and sesame seeds. In the mouth, flavors of boiled peanut, creamy coffee, and a touch of anise are soft and mild. The finish has a touch of caramel.

ZINACANTÁN PAPALOMETL 2021

Fabiola Torres Monfil, San Diego la Meza Tochimiltzingo, Puebla

Papalometl (**A. potatorum**)

ABV: 48%

PRICE: n/a

A treat to savor. ▪ Earthy almonds, soil, and flavorful citrus pith are rich aromas. The flavors echo on the palate with more citrus, guava, fresh cucumber, sugar snap peas, and honey. The finish is leafy and creamy at once.

ZINACANTÁN PECHUGA 2021

Fabiola Torres Monfil, San Diego la Meza Tochimiltzingo, Puebla

Papalometl (**A. potatorum**)

ABV: 47%

PRICE: n/a

Almost bourbon-like in its brown sugar and fruity richness. ▪ Aromas of mango, wet leaves, citrus, and chili all swirl together. On the palate, it is silky and unctuous, with plums, baked stone fruits, red chili, and vanilla custard.

RAICILLA, BACANORA & SOTOL

This section is made up of agave spirits that fall under their own subcategories: raicilla, a regional mezcal from Jalisco; bacanora, a regional mezcal from Sonora; and sotol, a mezcal-like spirit made from the dasylirion, or desert spoon plant, which is a close cousin of the agave. See page 44 for a more in-depth breakdown of these categories.

ESTANCIA

Rio Chenery founded Estancia Raicilla in 2014, following his own passion as well as a personal family history of appreciating the regional spirit of Jalisco. Among the first raicilla brands to hit the international market, the flagship spirit is made in the Sierra Madre Occidental, a mountainous region of Jalisco, as opposed to the coast. The brand has recently expanded to offer spirits from different producers across Jalisco, including a pechuga.

ESTANCIA RAICILLA
Alfredo Salvatierra, La Estancia, Jalisco
A. maximiliana

ABV: 45%
PRICE: $$

The flavors are interesting if a bit disjointed in some bottlings. ▪ Dried mint and tangerine peel aromas have a sunbaked quality to them. In the mouth, the dried herbs turned to stewed herbs, followed by eucalyptus and overripe lemon.

ESTANCIA PECHUGA

Alfredo Salvatierra, La Estancia, Jalisco

A. maximiliana

ABV: 48%

PRICE: $$

The first commercially available pechuga raicilla. Fermented in clay pots and distilled with local seasonal fruits and spices. ■ Fresh and crisp aromas are reminiscent of a sun-drenched field in a spring breeze. Mouth-drying tannins add a dynamic textural element, bringing to life flavors of lime leaf, oranges, and smoked ham.

ESTANCIA DESTILADO DE PULQUE

Alfredo Salvatierra, La Estancia, Jalisco

Manso (*A. salmiana*)

ABV: Unknown

PRICE: $$

Not technically a mezcal, this is distilled pulque from Tlaxcala. ■ Mango candy and paleta aromas are fun and very enticing. The texture is soft and creamy, like pulque. The flavor comes on sharp, with fermented black peppercorn, parmesan cheese rind, green mango, and limes. Fun, but not mezcal.

FLOR DEL DESIERTO

This Mexican-owned brand of sotol launched in 2011 and continues to be one of the strongest offerings of sotol from Chihuahua available today. The brand features distinct bottlings that celebrate the regional techniques of two producers and the terroir of Chihuahua. Their offerings include two pechugas, one of which contains rattlesnake.

FLOR DEL DESIERTO SOTOL DESERT
Gerardo Ruelas Hernandez, Chihuahua
Dasylirion leiophyllum

ABV: **45%**

PRICE: **$$**

Dark roasted flavors show off the versatility of sotol. ■ Minty and herbal aromas abound. Roasted flavors of baked earth, sal de gusano, and burnt orange are deep and caramelized flavors. The finish is chocolatey and bittersweet, with notes of roasted tobacco.

IZO

Izo bacanora is a new spirit from Izo Spirits, a California-based agave spirits company that offers everything from wood-aged mezcal to tequila. The unique group of co-founders include Durango native and entrepreneur Gaston Martinez, along with friend Linda Belzberg and her son Torrey. The brand was born from a desire to share a personal passion for Mexican culture with a wider audience through traditional spirits.

IZO BACANORA
Sonora
Pacifica (*A. angustifolia*)

ABV: 44%
PRICE: $$$

A touch harsh and lacking agave character, but fine overall. ▪ The aromas are slightly muddled, with notes of green herbs and overripe tropical fruit peeking through. The flavors hit quickly with gentle mint and pineapple before fading away to a raw alcohol finish.

LA HIGUERA

Owned by Esteban Morales of Derrumbes (page 145) and La Venenosa (page 216), this sotol brand was launched in 2018. The brand explores and features the different varieties of sotol, including cucharilla from Oaxaca and Puebla.

LA HIGUERA DASILYRION WHEELERI
Gerardo Ruelas Hernandez, Aldama, Chihuahua
Dasilyrion wheeleri

ABV: 48%
PRICE: $$

A clean and earthy sotol. ▪ Aromatically light, the flavor of this sotol is grounded in roasted artichoke, cucumber, and mochi. White tea mix with a hint of smoky leather, but do not overpower the plant essence.

LAS PERLAS DE JALISCO

Launched in 2018 by Nikhil Bahadur, founder and former owner of Blue Nectar Tequila (page 74), Las Perlas is co-owned by Nikhil and Jorge Luis Carbajal Díaz. Located in the coastal region for raicilla production, the family are well regarded in their community as fifth-generation producers of quality artisanal spirits, with nearly a century of knowledge passed down. One of the most unique aspects of their flagship spirit is an extended fermentation that lasts twenty to thirty days. The brand continues expansion to represent more of the local agave varieties, using a semi-wild/semi-cultivated approach on the hilly terrain.

LAS PERLAS DE JALISCO COSTA
Santiago Díaz Ramos, Las Guasimas, Jalisco
Amarillo, Verde (*A. angustifolia, A. rhodacantha*)

ABV: 48%	A spicy and clean raicilla. Sip on its own or pair with birria. ▪ Aromas are balanced between vegetal and floral notes. In the mouth, the flavor is spice-driven with green and red chili peppers, umami-rich sea salt, a touch of smoke, and roasted green bell peppers. The finish is uplifted by a hint of fruitiness.
PRICE: $$$	

LA VENENOSA

La Venenosa is a unique and important brand of agave distillates. The brand launched in the United States in 2014 by owner Esteban Morales, who also owns Derrumbes Mezcal (page 145) and Sotol La Higuera (page 214), and importer Arik Torren, co-owner of Fidencio Mezcal (page 158). La Venenosa was the first internationally available raicilla, and many of its spirits have been the first of their kind to be exported. The brand features different producers, offering a taste and insight into the variety of still types used in the state, including pre-industrial stills. Tasting through the lineup is an educational and sensory experience, and delightfully humbling to anyone who fancies themselves an expert in agave spirits.

LA VENENOSA RAICILLA AZUL
Don Guelo, La Estancia, Jalisco
Azul (*A. tequilana*)

ABV: 41.8%
PRICE: $$$$

Balanced and clean, this raicilla is made from the same agave variety used to make tequila. ■ The aromas are full of barbecue spice, orange zest, and butter. The flavors are clean and refreshing on the palate, with mineral-rich astringency and a meaty core with notes of pepperoni. Sweet and smoky paprika linger on the finish.

LA VENENOSA SIERRA DEL TIGRE
Luis Contreras, Manzanilla de la Paz, Jalisco
Bruto (*A. inaequidens*)

ABV: 46%
PRICE: $$$$

This raicilla undergoes a very long, dry fermentation, which is where the lactic funk comes from. ■ Parmesan cheese is salty and umami forward on the nose. While there is a lot of lactic funk in aroma and flavor, it is clean and crisp. There are fruity and floral undertones, showing mango and soursop. Miso and American cheese linger on the palate.

MEZONTE

See the profile for Valentin Cortés on page 155.

MEZONTE RAICILLA JAPO
Hildegardo Joya, Cabo Corrientes, Jalisco
Amarillo (*A. angustifolia*)

ABV: 46%

PRICE: $$$$

A unique mezcal made in small batches with a cult following. ■ Smokey aromas are full of marzipan, almond skin, and thyme. The flavors are sweet and piney, and burst with notes of cherry and almond. The texture is refined and velvety. The finish is luxuriously long and smooth and kissed with cinnamon.

ORIGEN RAÍZ

See the producer profile for Valentin Cortés on page 155.

ORIGEN RAÍZ SOTOL
Valentin Cortés, Tuitan, Durango
Dasylirion cedrosanum

ABV: 50%

PRICE: $$

Exceptional complexity in this sotol, which seems to get better and better with each release. ■ Aromas of earthy wet clay, orange peel, and lime. The flavors are complex and balanced, showing red chili spice and green plantain, and it has a silky texture. The finish is light with coffee notes.

RANCHO TEPUA

Previously known as Cielo Rojo, a brand that ultimately dissolved due to issues getting it to market. With more excitement in the agave spirits category, Rancho Tepua was first imported and launched by Arik Torren in 2017. Owned and produced by fifth-generation maestro Roberto Contreras, who works alongside his son Roberto Jr., the brand is very much a labor of love from this cattle ranching family. They use mostly estate-grown agaves and would be using 100% estate-grown agaves currently if not for the unprecedented frosts in Sonora two years in a row in 2010 and 2011, which killed much of the local crop. In addition to bacanora, they produce other agave spirits and Palmilla (a local variety of sotol).

RANCHO TEPUA BLANCO BACANORA

Roberto Contreras, Aconchi, Sonora
Pacifica (*A. angustifolia*)

ABV: 48%
PRICE: $$

Sweet and spicy. ■ Green fruit aromas have a touch of acetone. Chalky and sweet in the mouth, the flavors are very ripe with banana, chocolate, and hot cinnamon. It remains zesty on the finish as the green herbal notes turn roasted.

SANTO CUVISO

Santo Cuviso is a relatively new to market bacanora made by third-generation bacanorero Rumaldo Flores Amarillos, in partnership with the Oroz Coppel family, including the young Ana Sofia, who is the maestra bacanorera in training. Their current production is made from mostly wild agaves, with plans in the works to use 100% estate-grown agaves from the family ranch in the near future. Their offerings include a flagship bacanora, occasional limited releases made from carefully selected wild agaves, and spirits infused with local ingredients.

SANTO CUVISO BLANCO
Rumaldo Flores Amarillos, Bacanora, Sonora
Pacifica (*A. angustifolia*)

ABV: 45%
PRICE: $$

A boldly flavored bacanora with sweet and savory complexity. ■
The aromas are characterized by green vines and vegetation, sweet crisp asparagus picked fresh from the garden. The full body and rich flavors expand over the palate, showing off silky tropical fruit custard, citrus, and a touch of lactic tartness.

SANTO CUVISO UVALAMA
Rumaldo Flores Amarillos, Bacanora, Sonora
Pacifica (*A. angustifolia*)

ABV: 45%
PRICE: $$

Infused with the endemic uvalama fruit, like a cross between a sweet berry and stone fruit. ■ Diverse aromas of lactic sweetness and wild strawberry. The flavor is softened and gently sweet from the uvalama, which also imparts an amber tinge. Notes of peaches, herbs, and apricots stay fresh on the finish.

CHAPTER 5
COCKTAILS

My any people are first turned on to the world of agave spirits through cocktails. Tequila cocktails have long been in fashion and are universally loved, though the spirit has so much more to offer than a classic Margarita or vintage tequila sunrise. Today, agave spirits are featured in top cocktail bars around the world specifically because they play so well with a range of flavors. The complexity of agave spirits lends itself to mixing with both savory and sweet ingredients into drinks that can be silken or frothy. And it doesn't take much work; even a cocktail novice can create a drink that's enjoyable.

Making cocktails is a lot like cooking. The more you do it, the more comfortable you feel taking liberties to tailor recipes to your preferences and use what you have on hand. Above all, preparing cocktails at home is a creative and fun endeavor, and truly, it is very difficult to mess up. Use the guidelines and recipes included here for inspiration.

Select Your Spirits

A great cocktail will enhance the natural characteristics of a spirit, never cover them up, so always start with high-quality spirits you enjoy. When stocking your bar with agave spirits, I recommend including at least one unaged tequila, one aged tequila, and one mezcal to use for cocktails. Most cocktail recipes will recommend a certain type of spirit, but like preparing any food or drink, it can be fun to experiment to learn more about your drink preferences and even create your own recipes. You can play around with switching the base spirit between tequila and mezcal, or split the difference and include both!

TEQUILA

Tequila is a popular spirit for mixing into cocktails of all kinds. Both unaged and aged tequilas work in a wide range of recipes. When it comes to choosing which type of tequila to use, it can be helpful to think about the flavors you want to enhance—focusing on unaged bottles for crisp and earthy flavors, and on aged expressions for sweet, caramelized flavors. Just like cooking with wine, never use a tequila that you wouldn't sip straight; cocktails aren't meant to cover up unpleasant or harsh notes of a spirit, but rather to highlight their most delicious attributes.

Previous: Tequila Manhattan

MEZCAL

Traditionally, mezcal is not mixed into cocktails but enjoyed neat at room temperature. These cocktails started popping up within the last couple of decades, primarily as a way to introduce adventurous drinkers to the pungent spirit. Because the trend of mezcal cocktails is so prevalent now, there are more than a few brands that are specifically formulated mezcals for mixing. These spirits tend to be 45% ABV or lower and are more consistent batch to batch.

When it comes to artisanal batch mezcal, I tend to agree that it is best enjoyed unmixed. When in doubt, follow the guidelines that would be used for other spirit categories—treat your premium mezcal the way you would treat high-end single malt Scotch or extra-aged Armagnac. For those who want to experiment with specialty mezcal cocktails, I suggest using a less rare bottling and starting with simple flavor combinations.

RECOMMENDED SPIRITS FOR COCKTAILS

Siete Leguas Reposado Tequila

Fortaleza Añejo Tequila

Calle23 Blanco Tequila

Ocho Añejo Tequila

Partida Blanco Tequila

Cascahuín Blanco Tequila

Tapatio Blanco Tequila

Pueblo Viejo Blanco Tequila

Banhez Mezcal

El Guel, by Wahaka Mezcal

Cenizo Colonial, by Lágrimas
de Dolores Mezcal

Your Bespoke Bar

GLASSWARE

There are four kinds of basic glassware needed to accommodate any and all cocktails. From those basic categories, there are endless variations.

- **Stemmed glass:** Glasses that have a stem should be used for drinks that are served straight up—that is, without ice. Holding the glass by the stem ensures that the hands won't heat up the drink while it is being enjoyed.

- **Rocks glass:** A short and wide glass that accommodates approximately four ounces or less of a beverage, along with one large piece of ice.
- **Highball glass:** A tall glass is well-suited for drinks over four ounces in volume and long drinks that are topped with soda or another carbonated beverage. The shape of the glass encourages the bubbles to stay intact longer. These glasses also work for drinks that are made with crushed ice.
- **Mugs:** Use your favorite mugs for any warm or hot cocktail, such as a hot toddy.

TOOLS

I'm a big fan of using what you have already. For the most part, it's not necessary to buy expensive specialty accessories and equipment in order to make top-notch drinks. But if you do want to invest in a couple of bar tools, you won't need much.

- **Boston shaker:** The one accessory I think worth having on hand is a two-part shaker tin and pint glass. This is the shaker of choice in cocktail bars across the world because it is so versatile and can assist in the preparation of a variety of beverages. These shakers typically come with a strainer that fits the tin and the glass. Happily, the cheapest stainless-steel ones are usually the best industrial quality, so stick to the styles you see in bars rather than ones with design flair, which can often impair the functionality.
- **Jigger:** A standardized measuring utensil, or a jigger, is useful and typically comes double-sided, with either 1-ounce and 2-ounce or 0.75-ounce and 1.5-ounce measurements. If you don't have this tool, you can use anything in its place—a tablespoon, a shot glass, for example. The important part is to stay consistent with the ratios, rather than obsessing over specific measurements.
- **Muddler:** You probably don't need to own this bar tool to infuse fresh flavors into your cocktails. Anything that smashes can be a muddler—a can, a glass, a bean or potato masher—be resourceful and use your imagination.
- **Bar spoon:** A long spoon is convenient for stirring tall drinks. The twisted detail on a proper bar spoon will be necessary for anyone who wants to take their drink making to a professional level, as it allows you to layer in different liquids as well as add carbonated liquids without disrupting the liquids already in the glass. However, most standard-sized spoons will do the trick. You can also use a large kitchen spoon for batched drinks.

ICE

Ice is an important and often overlooked aspect of cocktails, especially when crafting at home. While it's not practical to have a state-of-the-art ice machine at home, it's easy to always have high-quality ice. Investing in a few silicone ice molds, specifically the 1-inch or 2-inch cubes or spheres, allows anyone to have bar-quality ice on hand. Remember: The bigger the ice, the slower it melts into the drink. I highly suggest buying the cube trays that come with a top to avoid the ice picking up freezer flavors. In advance of parties or gatherings, make a few trays per day and store the ice in a freezer bag to build up a ready-to-use stash.

SYRUPS

Making your own bespoke syrups is easy and greatly enhances the possibilities for at-home mixing. To make a simple syrup, combine equal parts water and sugar in a saucepan over medium-high heat until the sugar is fully dissolved into the water. It's that easy!

Variations include:

- **Herb-infused syrup:** Start with three sprigs of fresh herbs per 1 cup of simple syrup. Always add fresh herbs after the simple syrup is fully combined and the heat has been turned off. This prevents the herbs from cooking and preserves the freshness in the final flavor. Before adding, smack or slap the fresh herbs between your palms or against a hard surface to release some of their oils. Allow the herbs to steep, checking for the desired level of flavor intensity every 10 minutes. Once the flavor intensity is to your desired level, strain the simple syrup and store in an airtight container, ideally glass, in the fridge for up to 3 months.
- **Chili-infused syrup:** Slice the chilies in half in order to expose the ribs. If you don't want a spicy syrup, remove the ribs and seeds from the chilies before adding. The heat and flavor of fresh chilies varies greatly, but, in general, it's best to start with one or two chilies for each cup of simple syrup. Add the sliced chilies to the syrup immediately after the sugar dissolves and the heat is turned off. Taste the syrup for the desired level of spice every 5 minutes. Note that very hot chilies, like habanero, often infuse quite a bit of spice and flavor in under 10 minutes. It's difficult to follow guidelines, since chilies vary so widely in their level of spiciness—as does personal taste and tolerance—so treat each batch individually. Once the flavor intensity is to

your desired level, strain the simple syrup and store in an airtight container, ideally glass, in the fridge for up to 3 months.

- Spice-, tea-, or dried herb/fruit–infused syrup: Start with 2 teaspoons of ingredients per cup of simple syrup. Hard spices like star anise, clove, and cinnamon; roots like ginger or turmeric; and dried herbs and tea can be simmered in the simple syrup for 5 to 10 minutes just before turning the heat off. The longer you simmer, the more intense the flavor will be. This brief simmering ensures that all the flavors are fully released into the syrup. After the heat is turned off, allow the ingredients to steep, checking for flavor every 5 minutes. Once the flavor intensity is to your desired level, strain the simple syrup and store in an airtight container in the fridge for up to 3 months.

RIMS

Rimming a cocktail glass adds flavor and visual appeal and is an easy way to put a signature spin on any drink. In addition to the typical plain salt and chili salt, experiment with different kinds of salts like smoked salt, sal de gusano, and tajin (a classic blend of salt and chilies used all over Mexico). Adding sugar or cinnamon to salty and spicy rims can create even more depth of flavor. When adding cinnamon, sugar, or other spices to salt rims, start with equal parts spice and salt, then adjust for preference. Ingredients like citrus zest and any powdered herb can also be added to rims.

Think outside of the box and try pairing your rims with the ingredients or dish the cocktail will accompany. For example, if you are making a cocktail to accompany a barbecue, try using the dry rub to rim the glass.

In addition to getting creative with the rim mixture, the liquid you dip the glass in is also an opportunity for experimentation. Lime, orange, and pineapple juices all work well. Vinegar, chamoy, and simple syrup are less common options that can add intrigue to the overall flavor.

My preferred method of rimming a glass is to cut a slit in a piece of fruit and run it along the lip of a glass, or to dip the top lip of the glass into a shallow dish filled with the liquid base; then roll the moistened lip in the salt mixture. Rimming only half of the glass is the safest way to go, giving the drinker the option of taking a sip with or without the additional flavors imparted by the rim.

GARNISHES

Many cocktails are beautiful on their own, with or without a colorful rim, and may not require a garnish. That being said, using what you have on hand to enhance the overall presentation is another opportunity to create a signature drink.

A few tried-and-true garnish ideas:

- Fresh herb stalks such as rosemary, thyme, or basil; slap them between your palms or against a hard surface to release their oils, or torch them to create a pungent smokiness
- Cinnamon stick, torched to release a pungent smokiness
- Roasted or grilled fruit skewers
- Citrus wedges and wheels
- Citrus twists and peels, squeezed to release their oils over the top of the glass
- Colorful edible flowers such as orchids or nasturtium

Cocktail garnishes and rims are an easy way to introduce unexpected flavors and color to your cocktails.

CLASSIC COCKTAILS & ORIGINAL RECIPES

Opposite: A classic Margarita.

MARGARITAS

A classic margarita, although simple, is a masterpiece. Complemented with lime, salt, and a touch of sweetness, the agave spirit comes to life in all of its delicious layers of flavor. Margaritas are sours, meaning the basic building blocks will be 2 parts spirit, 1 part sour (lime/lemon), and 1 part sweet (liqueur, simple syrup, agave nectar, honey, maple syrup, etc.). Using this formula as a starting point makes it easy to customize drinks based on seasonal ingredients, flavor preferences, and what's on hand. Adjust the ratios to suit your tastes; for example, if you like your cocktails less sweet than average, consider knocking down the 1 part sweet to ½ or ¾ of a part instead of a full part. Using ratios as the building blocks also frees up the need for fancy bar equipment—use a shot glass, a teacup, or any other measuring vessel to create the ratios rather than obsessing over ounces.

Margaritas are shaken cocktails, which gives them a light and airy texture that adds to the overall refreshing quality. That being said, if you are making a large batch, punchbowl style, or simply feeling lazy, nothing bad has ever happened from stirring rather than shaking margarita ingredients together. Mixologists may cringe at this controversial tip, and it's true that the final product will lack that extra level of refinement that you expect from a craft cocktail bar, but the drink will still be delicious. If you do choose to omit the shaking process, be sure to stir over ice even if you serve your drinks straight up—this ensures the drink will be chilled and properly diluted.

ALL-PURPOSE MARGARITA

This basic recipe is inspired by Julio Bermejo's Tommy's Margarita, which highlights the flavor of the tequila and celebrates agave as the star. Once mastered, it can serve as the base for all kinds of margaritas. Simple, classic, and delicious.

Salt, for rim

2 ounces Siete Leguas blanco tequila

1 ounce fresh lime juice

¾ ounce simple syrup

Rim half of a rocks glass with salt and set aside. Shake the ingredients with ice to chill and dilute, and strain over fresh ice into the rimmed glass.

MEZCAL-RITA

Using a combination of tequila and mezcal creates a balanced agave flavor, while the sherry adds depth and richness to match the intensity of the mezcal.

Salt, for rim

1 ounce Blue Nectar blanco tequila

1 ounce Del Maguey Vida mezcal

½ ounce Lustau Pedro Ximénez sherry

1 ounce fresh lime juice

Colorful flower for garnish

Rim half of a rocks glass with salt and set aside. Shake the tequila, mezcal, sherry, and lime juice with ice to chill and dilute. Strain over fresh ice into the rimmed glass, and garnish with an orchid or other beautiful edible flower.

MANGITO SONIDERO MARGARITA

The combination of habanero and mango elevates the natural sweetness and spiciness of tequila. Frozen mango puree is easy to find at Latin grocery stores, or make your own by blending up mango flesh and just enough water to create a smooth puree. Tip: substitute 1½ ounces of water in place of the tequila to make a delicious nonalcoholic beverage, which makes a nice accompaniment to a copita of mezcal.

Chili salt, for rim

2 ounces Partida reposado tequila

2 ounces mango puree, fresh or thawed from frozen

1 ounce fresh lime juice

1 ounce habanero simple syrup

Dried mango, for garnish

Rim half of a rocks glass with chili salt and set aside. Shake the tequila, mango puree, lime juice, and simple syrup with ice to chill and dilute. Strain over fresh ice into the rimmed glass, and garnish with a dried mango skewer.

Opposite: Mangito Sonidero Margarita

PIÑA MARGARITA

Pineapple is a natural complement to anything agave-based. While it's nice to use fresh juices, this is one recipe where using store-bought pineapple juice works just as well.

Chili salt, for rim

2 ounces Pasote blanco tequila

2 ounces pineapple juice

1 ounce fresh lime juice

½ ounce simple syrup

Roasted or grilled pineapple, for garnish

Rim half of a rocks glass with chili salt and set aside. Shake the tequila, pineapple juice, lime juice, and simple syrup with ice to chill and dilute. Strain over fresh ice into the rimmed glass, and garnish with a caramelized pineapple skewer.

BOOZY BRAIN FREEZE

Is a frozen Margarita ever okay? Short answer: absolutely! The best Margarita slushies are made by taking your Margarita recipe of choice and throwing it in a blender. Sometimes I substitute blue curaçao—an azure-colored liqueur flavored with dried orange peel—for the sweetener to make blue frozen margaritas, because why not? Many cocktail bars also feature "fancy" slushie machines that churn out seriously delicious frozen drinks. The ones to avoid are the commercial machines that use bagged "margarita mix," a strange brew of chemicals that could double as a potent cleaning agent.

SMOKY GINGER MARGARITA

The flavors of this lightly sweet cocktail are subtle, yet richly layered. Ginger and the smoky lapsang souchong tea echo the natural flavors of mezcal.

2 ounces Banhez mezcal

¾ ounce Domaine de Canton ginger liqueur

1 ounce fresh squeezed lime juice

½ ounce lapsang souchong and fresh ginger simple syrup

Colorful flower, for garnish

Shake the mezcal, ginger liqueur, lime juice, and simple syrup with ice to chill and dilute. Strain over fresh ice into a rocks glass, and garnish with a beautiful edible flower.

POMEGRANATE MARGARITA

To feature the tartness of the fruit, be sure to use 100% unsweetened pomegranate juice for this recipe. If you find only sweetened or pomegranate juice cocktail, omit the simple syrup and instead use an additional ounce of the sweetened juice.

Cinnamon salt, for the rim

1 ounce Siete Leguas reposado tequila

1 ounce Cenizo Colonial mezcal

2 ounces unsweetened pomegranate juice

1 ounce fresh lime juice

1 ounce simple syrup

Torched cinnamon stick, for garnish

Rim half of a rocks glass with cinnamon salt and set aside. Shake the tequila, mezcal, pomegranate juice, lime juice, and simple syrup with ice to chill and dilute. Strain over fresh ice into the rimmed glass, and garnish with a freshly torched cinnamon stick.

ELOTE MARGARITA

The softly earthy and sweet flavors of corn from the Nixta corn liqueur are a natural match for the pungent flavors of mezcal. Elote and maguey flavors are deeply rooted in ancestral cuisine, making this a versatile cocktail to pair with traditional foods.

Smoked chili salt, for rim

2 ounces Montelobos espadín mezcal

1¼ ounces Nixta Licor de Elote

1 ounce fresh lime juice

Rim half of a rocks glass with smoked chili salt and set aside. Shake the ingredients with ice to chill and dilute. Strain over fresh ice into the rimmed glass.

Opposite: Pomegranate Margarita

SUMMER HERB MARGARITA

Bring out the herbal flavors of tequila and make the most of a flourishing summer herb garden by mixing up this drink with cilantro, parsley, basil, or thyme.

Herb salt, for rim

2 ounces Calle 23 blanco tequila

1 ounce fresh lime juice

1 ounce herb simple syrup

Herb sprigs, for garnish

Rim half of a rocks glass with herb salt and set aside. Shake the tequila, lime juice, and simple syrup with ice to chill and dilute. Strain over fresh ice into the rimmed glass, and garnish with plenty of fresh herb sprigs.

ROSEMARY-CRANBERRY HOLIDAY MARGARITA

This tart and herbaceous drink has wintry flavors that make it a great choice for holiday celebrations. If using sweetened cranberry juice cocktail, omit the simple syrup and add an extra ounce of cranberry juice cocktail.

Citrus salt, for rim

2 ounces Fortaleza reposado tequila

2 ounces unsweetened cranberry juice

1 ounce fresh lime juice

1 ounce simple syrup

Torched rosemary sprig, for garnish

Fresh or blistered cranberries, for garnish

Rim half of a rocks glass with citrus salt and set aside. Shake the tequila, cranberry juice, lime juice, and simple syrup with ice to chill and dilute. Strain over fresh ice into the rimmed glass, and garnish with a freshly torched rosemary sprig and a few cranberries.

Summer Herb Margarita

Easy Paloma

PALOMAS

The paloma is an iconic Mexican cocktail that combines tequila, grapefruit soda, and a touch of salt for a refreshing long drink. If you are looking to buy a grapefruit mixer for your palomas, I recommend Q Grapefruit, which strikes a balance between tart and sweet and eliminates the need for extra ingredients. Traditional Mexican grapefruit sodas like Jarritos are another option, though you'll want to add fresh lime juice to balance the sugariness. You can also make your own grapefruit soda out of fresh or bottled grapefruit juice and club soda, though it doesn't deliver the crispness of the classic soda-based drink.

EASY PALOMA

A simple recipe that is balanced and quick to make.

Salt, for rim

1½ ounces Don Fulano blanco tequila

1 (6.7 ounce) bottle Q Grapefruit mixer

Grapefruit wedge, for garnish

Rim half of a highball glass with salt and fill with ice. Pour the tequila and mixer over the ice, and garnish with grapefruit wedge.

MEZCAL PALOMA

Using mezcal instead of tequila adds a touch of smokiness and extra richness to the classic flavors.

Citrus salt, for rim

1½ ounces Convite espadín mezcal

1 (6.7 ounce) bottle Q Grapefruit mixer

Lime wedge, for garnish

Rim half of a highball glass with citrus salt and fill with ice. Pour the mezcal and mixer over the ice, and garnish with lime.

EARL GREY PALOMA

Bergamot and black tea create extra layers of citrus and fruity aromas.

1½ ounces Tequila Ocho blanco

1 ounce Earl Grey simple syrup

1 ounce freshly squeezed lime juice

Grapefruit-flavored seltzer

Lime wheel, for garnish

Fill a highball glass with ice. Pour the tequila, simple syrup, and lime juice over the ice, then mix and top with grapefruit-flavored seltzer. Garnish with a lime wheel.

SPICY PALOMA

Add a touch of spice by muddling hot green chilies, such as jalapeños or serranos.

Salt, for rim

1 green chili, split down the middle

1½ ounces Arette blanco tequila

1 (6.7 ounce) bottle Q Grapefruit mixer

Lime wedge, for garnish

Rim half of a highball glass with salt. Add cut chili to the glass and muddle. Fill the glass with ice. Pour the tequila and grapefruit mixer over the ice. Garnish with a lime wedge.

STIRRED & STRONG COCKTAILS

These silky drinks pack a punch, since almost all components contain some alcohol. They make nice pairings with cheese boards, rich stews, sauces, and cigars.

MEZCAL NEGRONI

A contemporary classic and my all-time favorite mezcal cocktail. Batch a bottle of this and bring it to parties to impress your friends, family, and hosts. Some people like to change the classic ratio to include 1½ parts mezcal to 1 part each of bitters and vermouth.

1 ounce La Luna cupreata mezcal

1 ounce Campari

1 ounce Martini & Rossi sweet vermouth

Orange peel, for garnish

Add one large ice cube to a rocks glass and set aside. Fill a mixing glass or other vessel with ice and add the mezcal, Campari, and sweet vermouth. Stir to chill and combine. Strain into the rocks glass over the large ice cube. Squeeze the orange peel oils over the top of the liquid, run the orange peel along the rim of the glass, and then sink the peel into the drink.

TEQUILA MANHATTAN

A robust, agave-forward añejo tequila is an easy and successful substitute for rye whiskey in this classic cocktail.

2 ounces Tequila Ocho añejo

1 ounce Martini & Rossi sweet vermouth

2 dashes Angostura bitters

Orange peel, for garnish

Fill a mixing glass or other vessel with ice and add the tequila, sweet vermouth, and bitters. Stir to chill and combine. Strain into a chilled glass. Squeeze the orange peel oils over the top of the liquid, run the orange peel along the rim of the glass, and then sink the peel into the drink.

Mezcal Negroni

ELOTERO

This drink highlights the sweetness of fresh corn, balanced by pungent and spicy sal de gusano. The result is a creamy corn-flavored drink, similar to a chilled atole. To make corn milk, blend and strain fresh sweet corn and/or grate corn cobs to collect the milky juice. Substituting other plant-based or dairy milks for the corn milk is fine, although some preservatives used in nut milks may cause some visible separation, and the drink will require stirring every so often.

Sal de gusano, for rim

2 ounces Vago Elote mezcal

2 ounces Nixta Licor de Elote

1 ounce corn milk

Rim a glass with sal de gusano and fill with ice. Pour the ingredients over the ice and stir to combine.

IT'S A BITTERSWEET LIFE

This combination is as delicious as it is easy to whip together.
Enjoy this drink as an aperitif or digestif.

½ ounce Vida mezcal

½ ounce Amaro Montenegro

Combine the ingredients in a glass and enjoy as a shot.

DESSERT COCKTAILS

Typically sweet and rich, dessert cocktails are meant to be the dessert rather than be paired with dessert. After indulging in one of these, you won't feel like you're missing out on a treat.

ESPRESSO MEZCALTINI

The espresso martini gets an upgrade from its already exalted status by replacing the neutral vodka with flavorful mezcal. This is hands down one of the tastiest mezcal cocktails that works well as dessert or a pregaming drink.

1 ounce Lágrimas de Dolores cenizo mezcal

1 ounce Mr. Black coffee liqueur

1 ounce cooled espresso

Espresso beans, for garnish

Add the mezcal, coffee liqueur, and espresso to a shaker with ice. Shake to chill and combine. Strain into a chilled coupe glass, and garnish with espresso beans.

FROZEN MEZCAL HOT CHOCOLATE

This is basically a boozy Mexican chocolate milkshake, so what's not to love?
The alcohol flavor is subtle, and it enhances the chocolate and cinnamon.

1 cup milk of choice

1 tablespoon unsweetened cocoa powder, plus extra for garnish

1½ ounces Cenizo Colonial mezcal

1½ ounces simple syrup

¼ ounce vanilla extract

¼ ounce cinnamon powder

Small pinch sea salt

1 cup ice

Whipped cream, for garnish

Combine all ingredients except the whipped cream in a blender and blend until smooth. Pour into a milkshake glass and top with cocoa powder and whipped cream.

COCONUT CREAMSICLE

This creamy cocktail evokes a childhood favorite with
soft flavors of orange, vanilla, and caramel.

1 ounce El Tesoro añejo tequila

1 ounce Tokaj Spirit Vegan Coconut and Almond Cream Liqueur

½ ounce Grand Marnier

Orange zest, for garnish

Add the tequila, coconut and almond cream liqueur, and Grand Marnier to a shaker with ice. Shake to chill and combine. Strain into a chilled coupe glass, and garnish with freshly grated orange zest.

Opposite: Frozen Mezcal Hot Chocolate

WARM COCKTAILS

Warm agave spirit cocktails have a way of feeling extra comforting and a touch medicinal, in a good way. There's nothing better to warm you up on a cold frosty day or night. As always with warm cocktails, you want to make sure the hot base isn't too hot. (If you can't sip it or stick your finger in it without burning yourself, it's too hot.) Always add the spirit last so the alcohol stays intact and won't vaporize.

AGAVE GINGER HOT TODDY

Spicy and warming, this all-purpose remedy cocktail can be enjoyed any time of day.

Hot water

1 ounce fresh lemon juice

1 ounce honey

½ ounce fresh ginger juice

1½ ounces La Gritona reposado tequila

Fill a mug with hot water. Add the remaining ingredients, putting in the tequila last. Stir to combine. Top with a slice of lemon, if desired.

MAPLE NETTLE HOT TODDY

This toddy celebrates the natural ingredients found in the northeastern part of the American continent: nettles and maple.

Hot water

Dried nettle leaves

1 ounce fresh lemon juice

1 ounce maple syrup

1½ ounces Mal Bien mezcal

Steep the nettle leaves in the hot water to make a tea. While still hot, add the remaining ingredients, putting in the mezcal last. Stir to combine.

Opposite: Agave Ginger Hot Toddy

SAVORY COCKTAILS

Savory cocktails are becoming more popular, and for good reason. Especially when it comes to agave spirits, the layers of umami and savoriness are often the characteristic traits that make them so uniquely delicious. These out-of-the-ordinary cocktail recipes are here to inspire signature cocktails that feature the less-explored flavors of agave.

MEZCAL SIPPING BROTH

Sipping broth is made even more soul-warming by spiking it with a little mezcal.

1 cup bone broth

1 ounce El Güel mezcal

Squeeze of fresh lemon juice

Finely diced onion, for garnish

Cilantro or parsley sprigs, for garnish

Add the mezcal to the hot bone broth. Squeeze in the lemon juice and top with the onion and herbs.

HEIRLOOM TOMATO HIGHBALL

This refreshing highball version of a Bloody Maria is a flavorful way to quench your thirst on a hot summer day. It is best prepared during the height of tomato season, when they are ripe and plentiful. Feel free to get creative with rims, mixers, and garnishes. Consider adding chopped fresh or powdered dried herbs, citrus zest, or other seasonings to the salt rim to customize the flavors. Use balsamic vinegar for a sweet and savory accent, or make it spicy by muddling fresh chilies in the bottom of the glass.

Sherry vinegar, for rimming the glass

Salt and pepper, for rimming the glass

2 ounces tomato puree, about half a medium-to-large heirloom tomato with skin removed

2 ounces Tapatío blanco tequila

1 ounce lime juice

Seltzer

Fresh basil, for garnish

Dip the rim of a highball glass in the sherry vinegar, then in salt and pepper. Fill the glass with ice. Add the tomato puree, tequila, and lime juice, then top with seltzer. Garnish with fresh basil.

BARTENDER SPOTLIGHT: SPECIALTY COCKTAILS

This selection of cocktails from Mexican bar professionals represents the new wave of agave spirit mixology, informed by the culture and heritage of flavors from across different states of Mexico. Drinking these carefully crafted cocktails is a pure joy, but so is having a seat at their bar so you can listen to the stories and insights about the spirits they pour.

ONE WAY TO OAXACA

Julio Xoxocotla

Mexico-born Julio is a partner and head bartender at the Wild Son and Bar Lula in New York City. The phrase that inspired this fruity, lightly smoked, spicy and herbal cocktail is *"El dinero, el amor, y las guayabas no se pueden ocultar"*—in English, "Money, love, and guavas cannot be hidden."

1½ ounces Pelotón de la Muerte mezcal

1 ounce guava puree

¾ ounce Jalapeño-Rosemary Syrup (see page 274)

¾ ounce lime juice

Add all ingredients to a shaker. Add ice and shake well. Once cold, strain over fresh ice in a rocks glass.

MISS RUDA

Carmen López Torres

Carmen López Torres, who grew up in Mexico City and studied food chemistry there, consults with agave spirits companies and is always looking for new ways to use classic spirits. The Miss Ruda is a riff on a white negroni and was a fun mixology challenge for Carmen because the selection of amaros and aperitivos in Mexico is limited. You can find mezcal infused with ruda, a bitter herb, from the brand Mezcalillera. Otherwise, you can infuse espadín mezcal with ruda and still get the wonderful flavors of the plant.

1 ounce Lillet Blanc

¾ ounce mezcal espadín

½ ounce yellow chartreuse

¼ ounce ruda mezcal

4 dashes citric acid solution

2 dashes orange bitters

1 Red Ice Cube (see page 274)

Lemon peel, for garnish

Ruda or other green herb, for garnish

Add the Lillet, mezcal espadín, chartreuse, ruda mezcal, citric acid solution, and bitters to a mixing glass. Fill the glass with ice and stir until well chilled. Strain into a chilled rocks glass and add one Red Ice Cube. Express a lemon peel and roll it carefully along the rim of the glass, and then place in the glass. Garnish with a piece of ruda or another small green herb.

UXMAL CITY

Edgar Hernandez

Edgar is the head bartender at Freemans Restaurant in New York City. The name of this nutty, spicy, and citrusy cocktail is in reference to an ancient Mayan city located in the Eastern peninsula in the state of Yucatán, known for its intricate architecture, which includes a 100-foot-tall pyramid.

1½ ounces Pelotón mezcal

¼ ounce agave nectar

¼ ounce simple syrup

¼ ounce Ancho Reyes chili liqueur

¼ ounce blood orange puree

¼ ounce freshly squeezed lime juice

½ teaspoon allspice dram

Lime wheel sprinkled with chili, for garnish

Absinthe atomizer spray, for garnish

Add the mezcal, agave nectar, simple syrup, chili liqueur, blood orange puree, lime juice, and allspice dram to a shaker with ice. Shake to chill and combine, then strain over fresh ice into a rocks glass. Garnish with a lime chili wheel and spritz with absinthe.

TIME IN TULUM

Bryant J. Orozco

Bryant is a Los Angeles native and a proud descendant of Sonoran, Nayarita, and Zacatecano ancestry. A lifelong interest in learning about his heritage became intertwined with his career as a bartender and then as a curator of Mexican wine and spirits. When not pouring over books and spirits, he is traveling off the beaten path in Mexico. "This drink was created during the pandemic, when I had to create cocktails that were easy to make in a to-go format. The name pokes fun at the many people who reminisce about their 'time in Tulum.'"

1½ ounces mezcal (preferably a robust espadín)

½ ounce dry curaçao (I prefer Pierre Ferrand dry curaçao)

1 ounce cold-brewed Tamarind Syrup (see page 275)

½ ounce fresh lime juice

¼ ounce Agave Syrup (see page 274)

Pinch of salt

Splash of seltzer

Place the mezcal, curaçao, Tamarind Syrup, lime juice, Agave Syrup, and salt into a Boston shaker. Give it a medium shake to chill, but don't overdilute the drink. Fill a glass with fresh ice, add a splash of soda water, and pour the contents of the shaker over top. If you find the drink is too tart, add more agave. If it is too sweet for your taste, omit the agave syrup.

MÁQUINA VERDE

José María Dondé Rangel

Mexico City native José María is the founder of @panoramamezcal on Instagram and the beverage director at Claro Restaurant in Brooklyn, New York, a Michelin-starred destination that celebrates the culinary heritage of Oaxaca and carries an impressive selection of hard-to-find mezcal. In addition to tending bar in Brooklyn, he is known for pop-up bartender events across the eastern US, particularly in Miami and Washington, DC. For this multilayered herbaceous cocktail, José María took his inspiration from the poem "Romance Sonámbulo" by the twentieth-century Spanish poet Federico García Lorca: "Green, how I want you green. / Green wind. Green branches. / The ship out on the sea / and the horse on the mountain."

1½ ounces El Buho mezcal

½ ounce green chartreuse

1 ounce cucumber juice

¾ ounce lime juice

½ ounce Coconut-Basil Cream (see page 274)

3 dashes fresh chili serrano juice

1 slice cucumber, for garnish

Serrano Salt (see page 275), for garnish

Combine the mezcal, chartreuse, cucumber juice, lime juice, Coconut-Basil Cream, and chili serrano juice in a shaker with ice. Shake hard, strain into a highball glass over fresh ice, and garnish with a cucumber slice dipped in Serrano Salt.

PICOSITO

Elaine Romero

Elaine, head bartender at The Cabinet in New York City, likes to tell stories
about the spirits she serves, whether poured neat or crafted into cocktails
such as her Picosito. This cocktail combines agave with tropical flavors of
mango brandy and pineapple liqueur. What started as a hobby is now a passion.
Elaine has quickly become one of the nation's top agave bartenders.

Sal de gusano, for rimming the glass

1⅕ ounces Rey Campero Espadín mezcal

½ ounce jalapeño-infused tequila

½ ounce Rhine Hall Mango Brandy

**¾ ounce Turmeric-Ginger Honey Syrup
(see page 275)**

¾ ounce fresh lemon juice

¼ ounce cane syrup

**2 bar spoons Giffard Caribbean Pineapple
liqueur**

Rosemary sprig, for garnish

Rim a glass with sal de gusano and set aside.
Add the mezcal, tequila, brandy, Turmeric-
Ginger Honey Syrup, lemon juice, cane syrup,
and pineapple liqueur to a shaker with ice.
Shake to combine and chill. Strain into the salt-
rimmed glass and garnish with a rosemary sprig.

OAXACA EXPRESS

Alex Valencia

Alex is celebrated as one of the top Mexican mixologists of our time, and this drink is a cult favorite at La Contenta and La Contenta Oeste, the restaurants he co-owns in New York City. Alex created this cocktail back in 2009 before mezcal went mainstream and initially called it the Mexican Connection. "Back then, the mezcal in New York City was only exported from Oaxaca, so I changed the name to Oaxaca Express, like a little taste from Oaxaca, Mexico," he says.

Tajin, for rimming the glass

1 slice jalapeño, no seeds

2 ounces espadín mezcal from Oaxaca

¾ ounce Cucumber Puree (see page 274)

¾ ounce fresh lime juice

¾ ounce Agave Syrup (see page 274)

Rim a rocks glass with tajin and set aside. Add the jalapeño to a shaker and muddle, then add the mezcal, cucumber puree, lime juice, and agave syrup, plus ice. Shake for 5 to 7 seconds. Double strain and serve.

CHACMOOL HIBOL

Kami Kenna

Kami—a bartender, brand owner, consultant, and distiller—splits her time between Mexico and Peru. She designs beverages and beverage experiences to drive positive change in the producer communities of Latin America. Kami created the Chacmool Hibol in collaboration with In Situ bar in Oaxaca for a local bartender training program. Chacmool are pre-Columbian sculptures found throughout Mesoamerica. They are recognizable for their signature backward reclining posture and a vessel balanced on their bellies. "They are especially prevalent at Chichen Itza in the Yucatán Peninsula, where the anise-laced fermented honey Xtabentún liquor originates," says Kami. She recommends pairing a Chacmool Hibol with the short story "Chac Mool" by Carlos Fuentes.

1¼ ounces Versus Destilado de Agave con Chocolate

1¼ ounces sweet vermouth

¼ ounce Xtabentún

1 dash Angostura Bitters

Tonic water, to taste

Orange wheel, for garnish

Add the Versus Chocolate, vermouth, Xtabentún, and bitters to a mixing glass, add ice, and stir to chill. Strain the chilled ingredients into a highball glass filled with ice and top off with tonic water. Be sure to stir the ingredients with a bar spoon to integrate the spirits with the tonic water. Express an orange peel carefully around rim of the glass and then place it in the drink.

LA PENCA

Andre Levon

Andre is the bar director of Bar Clavel in Baltimore, Maryland. His cocktail came to him in a dream one night when he was visiting a town just outside of Tuito, Jalisco. The flavors are meant to emphasize the overripe fruit characteristic of the raicilla that originates from the Sierra Madre Occidental. Andre uses panela sugar for his simple syrup, which can be purchased at specialty food stores.

1¾ ounces La Venenosa Raicilla Sierra Occidental

¾ ounce mature pineapple juice

¾ ounce lime juice

½ ounce Tempus Fugit Banane

½ ounce panela simple syrup

Pineapple leaf, for garnish

Add the raicilla, pineapple juice, lime juice, banana liqueur, and simple syrup to a shaker with ice. Shake to chill and combine, strain over 4 to 6 cubes of fresh ice into a rocks glass, and garnish with a pineapple leaf. Serve with a straw.

EL ARDIDO

Elvis Pinelo

Elvis hails from Santa Cruz Etla Oaxaca, Mexico, but left Oaxaca from a very young age with his parents, who relocated to the Hudson Valley in New York. He can be found in his family owned restaurant La Cabanita in Poughkeepsie, New York, which boasts the most extensive collection of agave spirits in the region. El Ardido—which translates to burned, irritated, or even bold and daring—is in reference to the layers of spicy ingredients, especially chile de arbol, which is one of the hottest typical dried chilies in Mexican cuisine. All of the bold ingredients in the cocktail are meant to highlight the naturally spicy quality of the tepextate agave.

Chamoy, for rimming the glass

Tajin, for rimming the glass

1 (1 inch) peeled pineapple chunk

1 chile seco de árbol

1½ ounces El Mero Mero Tepextate mezcal

1 ounce pineapple juice

¾ ounce fresh lime juice

1 bar spoon Agave Syrup (page 274)

Rim a highball glass with chamoy and tajin and set aside. Muddle the pineapple chunk and chili in the bottom of a shaker and add ice. Add the mezcal, pineapple juice, lime juice, and agave syrup. Shake to combine and chill, then strain over fresh ice.

Specialty Cocktail Mixers

AGAVE SYRUP

Combine equal parts hot water and agave nectar and stir until thoroughly combined, approximately 1 to 2 minutes. The syrup will last a month when refrigerated.

COCONUT-BASIL CREAM

½ ounce coconut cream
Basil leaves

Blend the coconut cream with basil leaves to taste, and strain.

CUCUMBER PUREE

Cut one English cucumber into slices and puree in a blender.

JALAPEÑO-ROSEMARY SYRUP

7 jalapeños (3 without seeds)
2 sprigs rosemary (No stems, just leaves)
1 quart water
1 quart agave nectar

See page 225 for instructions to prepare this and other infused syrups.

RED ICE CUBE

¾ ounce Campari
2¼ ounces water
3 hibiscus leaves
2 dashes Peychaud's Bitters

Combine the Campari, water, and hibiscus leaves to a glass and let sit in the refrigerator overnight. The following day, add the Peychaud's Bitters. Pour the mixture into an ice cube tray and freeze.

SERRANO SALT

1 part Serrano chiles
1 part Maldon salt
1 part sugar

Dehydrate the serrano chiles with Maldon salt and sugar in a dehydrator, alternatively, use an herb grinder to blend dried chilies with salt and sugar, then adjust to taste.

TAMARIND SYRUP

15 freshly shelled tamarind pods
½ cup simple syrup (ideally made with piloncillo or brown sugar)

Place the tamarind pods in 1 liter of room-temperature water and let soak for 8 to 10 hours. Pour the tamarind pods and water through a sieve or strainer into a new container. With the back of a spoon, press the pods against the remaining pulp to separate the veins, pits, and any leftover shells. Pour the tamarind water over the veins and pits again to wash away any excess tamarind for the syrup. Add the simple syrup to the pulpy tamarind water, to taste. The flavor should be tart and sweet. You can store the syrup up to 3 weeks in the refrigerator. It also makes a great quick tamarind agua fresca.

TURMERIC-GINGER HONEY SYRUP

1 ounce ginger root, peeled and chopped
1 turmeric root, peeled and chopped
2 cups honey

Place the ginger root and turmeric root into 1 cup of hot water and mix. Strain with a cheesecloth or a fine strainer, and discard the solids. Add the honey to the liquid and mix. Store in a glass container in the refrigerator for up to 2 weeks.

ACKNOWLEDGMENTS

My deepest gratitude is toward the many families and communities across Mexico that have opened their distilleries, restaurants, bars, and homes to me—it is thanks to you that we get to enjoy agave spirits at all. To Asis Cortés, German Gutiérrez Gamboa, and Martha Garza in particular, I am eternally grateful for your continued friendship and generosity. I would like to thank all of the producers, brand owners, and representatives who took time to speak with me and send me samples in preparation for this project, during the height of a pandemic, no less. Likewise, to my friends and colleagues who helped edit the many sections of this book on short notice, I extend sincere appreciation for your support. A special thanks is due to Sabrina Lessard for her careful review of the manuscript, Susan Coss for lending her vast knowledge, Fabiola Santiago Hernández for her insight and perspective on the culture of mezcal, and to Kami Kenna for her valuable contributions to the distillation sections. Last, but certainly not least, thanks to Paul Pacult, for your friendship and guidance, and for paving the path I am lucky enough to walk along.

Opposite: The delivery of 15 tons of agave harvested from their own fields and that will become Tequila Fortaleza.

GLOSSARY

ABV: Alcohol by volume, measures the amount of ethanol by volume in a liquid. The alcohol by volume is half the amount of the spirit's "proof." For example, a 50% ABV spirit is 100 proof.

AGUAMIEL: The sweet sap from the agave plant, or the unfermented base of pulque.

AGUAVINO: The liquid produced after the first distillation.

BACANORA: A DO-protected agave spirit from Sonora, under the historical umbrella term mezcal, but with its own regional history, traditions, and culture.

BAGASO/GABASO: The fibers from crushed cooked agave.

BOTANA/BOTANEAR: A snack; to snack.

CABALLITO: A tall shot glass traditionally used for Tequila.

CAPON: An agave that has its quiote cut off in order to accumulate sugars in the heart.

CARRIZO: A bamboo-like plant used in mezcal production and to assess alcohol level by way of perlas.

CHAPULINES: Fresh, dried, or toasted grasshoppers, a traditional Oaxacan snack.

COA: A sharp circular ax used to cut the pencas off of the agave hearts.

COLAS: The tales, or last part of the distillate.

COMITECO: A regional spirit from Chiapas based on aguamiel fermented with mother yeast and piloncillo, then double distilled.

COPITA: A small cup from which to drink mezcal.

CUERPO/CORAZÓN: The body/heart, or middle part, of the distillate.

DENOMINATION OF ORIGIN (DO): A designation that applies to products from a certain region, typically encompassing specific traditions and methods of production that are customary to that geographic region.

DIXEEBE: A Zapotec term that expresses gratitude to all beings and circumstances that make a special moment possible.

FABRICA: A mezcal production facility, often adjacent to the producer's home.

HACIENDA: A large estate, usually with colonial roots and heritage.

JICARA: A half of a gourd used as a mezcal drinking vessel.

JIMADOR: A person who harvests and prepares agaves for cooking.

MAGUEY: Agave.

MAYAHUEL: An Indigenous teotl or embodied energy of the maguey spirit and plant.

METL: Agave.

MEZCAL: Agave; cooked agave; spirit made from agave.

MIXTO: A style of tequila made from less than 100% agave base material.

NAHUATL: The language of the Indigenous Nahua people.

NOM/NORMA: Mexican government-sanctioned standards or rules of production and allowed parameters of products or processes.

ORDINARIO: The liquid produced after the first distillation.

PALENQUE: A mezcal production facility, often located adjacent to a producer's home.

PECHUGA: A special type of mezcal with the last distillation including a house recipe that typically includes seasonal fruits, rice, spices, and an animal or part of an animal. This type of mezcal is typical for special occasions and comes from the heart, thus the symbolic inclusion of the breast, or pechuga of an animal.

PENCA: Leaves of the maguey.

PERLAS: The bubbles that form when using a jicara and carrizo set to judge the alcohol of a mezcal. From visually assessing these bubbles, or pearls, experienced producers can ascertain alcohol levels with the same precision as Western scientific devices.

PETATE: A woven straw mat from Indigenous cultures.

PIÑA: The heart of the agave, which bears a resemblance to a pineapple.

PULQUE: The Indigenous beverage of fermented aguamiel.

PUNTAS: The heads, or first part, of the distillate.

QUIOTE: The flowering stalk of the agave.

RAICILLA: A DO-protected agave spirit from Jalisco, under the historical umbrella term mezcal, but with its own regional history, traditions, and culture.

SAL DE GUSANO: A spiced salt made from chile, salt, and dried agave worms that is typically served alongside mezcal with fruit.

SOTOL: An artisanal Mexican-made spirit made from the sotol plant that is culturally similar to mezcal.

TABERNA: A mezcal production facility, often adjacent to the producer's home.

TAHONA: A large stone wheel pulled by a donkey, mule, or horse, used to crush cooked agave into a juicy pulp.

TEMAZCAL: An Indigenous practice in which red-hot rocks are placed on the earth in the center of a hut where participants sit in a circle and go through spiritual and cleansing rituals.

TEOTL: Metaphorical embodied natural energies, often mistranslated as gods or goddesses.

TEPACHE: A fermented beverage made from pineapple husks and seasoned with a variety of spices; the fermenting liquid from cooked agave.

TEQUILA: A DO-protected agave spirit from Jalisco, under the historical umbrella term mezcal, but with its own regional history, traditions, and culture.

VELADORA: A small glass candle holder, often used as a vessel to drink mezcal.

VINATA: A mezcal production facility, often adjacent to the producer's home.

REFERENCE GUIDE
& FURTHER READING

In addition to checking the websites of your favorite producers and brands, the resources listed below are options for diving in deeper.

In my experience, the best way to go deeper in your learning is to listen to the people who have the tradition of making mezcal. In the industry many of our relationships with people from Mexico who facilitate access to mezcal are not from the lineage of people who carry this traditional knowledge. That's not a moral critique, but a fact, since we mostly interface with owners or representatives of brands; it's a special treat when someone from a producer family is in town. Whenever you have the opportunity to listen to someone who is directly from the tradition, do it! There are first generation distillers all over Mexico, and the ones who are finding the most success have invested a lot of time with the original knowledge keepers.

Sustainability Issues, Educational Organizations & Mutual Aid Initiatives

- Bat Friendly: BatFriendly.org
- Film: *The Bat Man of Mexico: Rodrigo Medellín*, BBC Natural World, 2014
- Darcy Tetreault, Cindy McCulligh, and Carlos Lucio, "Distilling Agro-Extractivism: Agave and Tequila Production in Mexico," *Journal of Agrarian Change*, 2021.
- Arbolution in Oaxaca: TinySeedProject.org
- ICollective
- People & Plants: PeopleAndPlants.org
- Milpa AC: @milpa.ac
- Tequila Interchange Project: http://www.tequilainterchangeproject.org
- Centro de Estudios Sobre el Maguey y Mezcal AC: https://cemmez.org.mx
- Mi Oaxaca: @Mi.Oaxaca
- Proyecto LAM: https://realminero.com.mx/proyecto-lam

Previous: A blue agave field in Jalisco.

History of Distillation

- Daniel Zizumbo-Villareal et al., "Distillation in Western Mesoamerica before European Contact," Economic Botany 63, no. 4 (2009): 413–426.

Regulations & Laws

- Tequila DO current info: https://www.crt.org.mx/index.php/en
- CRM history and updates: Mezcalistas.com, ClaytonSzczech.com

Books

Bowen, Sarah. *Divided Spirits: Tequila, Mezcal, and the Politics of Production.* Oakland: University of California Press, 2015.

Bruman, Henry J. *Alcohol in Ancient Mexico.* Salt Lake City: University of Utah Press, 2008.

Carducci, Tad, and Paul Tanguay, with Alia Akkam. *The Tippling Bros.: A Lime and a Shaker.* Eugene, OR: Harvest, 2015.

Cooper, Ron. *Finding Mezcal: A Journey into the Liquid Soul of Mexico.* New York: Ten Speed Press, 2018.

Dunbar-Ortiz. *An Indigenous Peoples' History of the United States.* Boston: Beacon Press, 2015.

Fernández, Rodolfo, and José Luis Vera Cortés. *Agua de las verdes matas: Tequila y mezcal.* Mexico City: Conaculta, 2015.

Gaytán, Marie Sarita. *¡Tequila! Distilling the Spirit of Mexico.* Stanford, CA: Stanford University Press, 2014.

Gentry, Howard. *Agaves of Continental North America.* Tucson: University of Arizona Press, 2004.

González, Roberto J. *Zapotec Food: Farming and Food in the Northern Sierra of Oaxaca.* Austin: University of Texas Press, 2001.

Greene, Granville. *The Mezcal Rush: Explorations in Agave Country.* Berkeley, CA: Counterpoint, 2017.

Hooker, Juliet. *Black and Indigenous Resistance in the Americas.* Washington, DC: Lexington Books, 2020.

Lemus, América Minerva Delgado. *Mezcalla: Tradición y cultura del mezcal michoacano.* Mexico City: Universidad Autónoma Metropolitana, 2021.

Long, Janet. *Conquista y comida consecuencias del encuentro de dos mundos, 3rd ed.* Mexico City: Universidad Nacional Autónoma de México Instituto de Investigaciones Históricas, 2018.

Martineau, Chantal. *How the Gringos Stole Tequila.* San Antonio, TX: Trinity University Press, 2015.

Moore, Jeff. *Agaves: Species, Cultivars, Hybrids.* Jeff Moore, 2021.

Nuñez, Joaliné Pardo, et al. *Miradas femeninas desde el mezcal.* Mexico: Centro de Investigación y Asistencia en Tecnología y Diseño del Estado de Jalisco, 2022.

Oyarzábal, Iván Saldaña. *The Anatomy of Mezcal.* N.p.: 2013.

Pacult, F. Paul. *The New Kindred Spirits.* Dallas: BenBella Books, 2021.

Pierce, Gretchen. *Alcohol in Latin America: A Social and Cultural History.* Tucson: University of Arizona Press, 2014.

Schroeder, James. *Understanding Mezcal.* Chicago: Prensa Press, 2019.

Torrentera, Ulises. *Mezcalaria: The Cult of Mezcal.* N.p.: Ediciones Farolito, 2018.

Townsend, Camilla. *Fifth Sun: A New History of the Aztecs.* New York: Oxford University Press, 2019.

Websites

- Tequila Matchmaker: tequilamatchmaker.com
- Mezcalistas: Mezcalistas.com
- Mezcal Reviews: MezcalReviews.com
- Experience Agave: ExperienceAgave.com
- Clayton Szczech: ClaytonSzczech.com
- ¡Hey Hey! Agave: https://tuyo.nyc/blogs/hey-hey-agave
- Maestros del Mezcal: MaestrosDelMezcal.com
- Ultimate Beverage Challenge: Ultimate-Beverage.com
- Mezonte: Mezonte.com
- Drink a Seat: DrinkASeat.com
- Mezcal PhD: MezcalPhD.com
- Mezcaleando: Mezcaleando.com
- Mezcología: Mezcologia.mx
- Sip Tequila: SipTequila.com
- MiOaxaca: MiOaxaca.com

Products

- Tuyo Agave Variety ID Cards
- Tuyo Mezcal Copitas
- 33 Copitas de Mezcal Tasting Booklets
- 33 Caballitos de Tequila Tasting Booklets
- Mezsalts
- La Rifa Chocolate
- Colectivo Bagatech

TESS'S TOP TEQUILAS & MEZCALS

TOP 10
TEQUILAS

Cascahuín Blanco

Don Fulano Blanco Fuerte

Tapatio Blanco

Fuenteseca Blanco Cosecha 2018

ArteNOM 1414 Reposado

Fortaleza Reposado Winter Blend

Ocho Reposado 2018 El Bajío

Siete Leguas Reposado

Storywood Speyside 7 Reposado

Partida Añejo

TOP 7
VALUE TEQUILA BRANDS

Cascahuín

El Tesoro

Partida

Calle 23

Don Fulano

ArteNOM

Siete Leguas

TOP 15
MEZCALS

Pal'alma Salmiana

Don Mateo Pechuga

Lágrimas de Dolores Verde

Lalocura Cuishe Espadín

La Luna Bruto

La Medida Tepeztate

Mezonte Candido

Real Minero Becuela

Rey Campero Mexicano

Tosba Tepextate

Lamata Tepemete Durango

Dixeebe Tobala

Alipús San Juan XX

Chacolo Ixtero Verde

Cuish Capon 2004

TOP 7
VALUE MEZCAL BRANDS

Lágrimas de Dolores

Sacro Imperio

Vago

La Luna

Don Amado

Banhez

Nuestra Soledad

IMAGE CREDITS

Title page: Credit: Courtesy of Mezcal Rey Campero
Dedication page: Jorge Tirado
Pages 8: Courtesy of Tepeztate La Medida
Page 10: Courtesy of Siete Leguas
Pages 12–13: Courtesy of Pal'alma Salmiana
Page 14: Tess Rose Lampert
Page 18: Courtesy of Siete Leguas
Page 19 Courtesy of La Luna Bruto
Pages 24–25: Courtesy of ArteNOM Tequila
Page 27: Jorge Tirado
Page 29: Azucena San Martín
Page 32: Courtesy of La Luna Bruto
Page 36: Courtesy of Siete Leguas
Page 37 (Top): Alfredo Martinez/Getty Images
Page 37 (Bottom): Matt Morrison
Pages 52–53: Courtesy of Pal'alma Salmiana
Pages 56–57: Courtesy of ArteNOM Tequila
Page 58: Shutterstock.com
Page 61: Sarah Jun
Pages 66–67: Courtesy of Siete Leguas
Page 68: Michael DeFreitas Central America/Alamy Stock Photo
Pages 122–123: Courtesy of La Luna Bruto
Page 124: Courtesy of La Luna Bruto
Pages 220–221: Sarah Jun
Page 227 (left): Winfried Heinze/Stockfood
Page 227 (right): The Picture Pantry/Stockfood
Page 228: Valerie Janssen/Stockfood
Pages 231, 232: Sarah Jun
Page 235: Courtesy of Instagram @JustSabrinaGali
Pages 236, 239, 240, 244, 247, 248, 251, 252, 255, 257, 261, 262, 265, 266, 268, 271, 272: Sarah Jun
Page 277 ©Tequila Fortaleza 2021
Page 278 from left: iStock/Getty Images Plus/Gettyimages.com
Page 279: Tess Rose Lampert
Page 280 from left: Courtesy of Siete Leguas; REAL MINERO BECUELA
Page 281 from left: Romana Lilic/Gettyimages.com; Tess Rose Lampert
Pages 282–283: Showing the world/Gettyimages.com
Pages 288–289: Arturo Ochoa/Gettyimages.com

Previous: A blue agave field in Jalisco.

PRODUCER-OWNED MEZCAL BRANDS

INDEX

Note: Page numbers in *italics* indicate/include photos.

ABOUT THE AUTHOR

Tess Rose Lampert's connection with Mexican culture began in early childhood. Thanks to a public elementary school immersion program, Tess learned about the many Indigenous populations of what is today Central and South America starting at five years old, with all schooling in Spanish taught by native speakers. She continued her studies throughout her university majors in linguistics and philosophy, specializing in Mayan glyphs, and dispelling the myth of contemporary portrayals of Mesoamerican nations as less civilized than their European counterparts. Shortly after completing a master's degree in philosophy of aesthetic taste, she began working in the wine and spirits industry. In the mid 2000s her work with spirits and lifelong appreciation for Indigenous culture overlapped as she learned about mezcal directly from producers in Mexico. At the same time, mezcal was becoming a trend in the international cocktail scene. Tess has dedicated a good deal of her professional life to agave education in an effort to breed appreciation for what is first and foremost an extension of culture, and to center the communities behind agave spirits. Known for her sharp palate, in addition to educational writings and events, she is a wine and spirits judge, and has her own consulting company, PalateTrip LLC.